EXPOSING FALSE DOCTRINE IN THE CHURCH

CINDY ROBERTSON HALL

Exposing False Doctrine in the Church

ISBN: 978-1-949106-91-6

Published by Word and Spirit Publishing
P.O. Box 701403
Tulsa, Oklahoma 74170
wordandspiritpublishing.com

Printed in the United States of America.

God's Plan

He sent His only
Son to earth...
of whom a virgin
did give birth,
that His Son,
sent from above,
would spread the message
of His love.
For the cross
Christ did bear
that the Kingdom
we all might share.
'Cause God's plan
should be fulfilled
that all men have
a chance to live.
And by Christ's death,
all our sins
if we repent
shall be cleansed.
So, from the truth
do not part.
Receive the Holy Spirit
with an open heart.
And in Jesus' name,
please do pray
so that you're prepared
on Judgment Day.

Contents

Introduction vii

1 Once Saved, Always Saved? 1

2 No Need to Repent after Salvation—Really? 9

3 God Chooses Some for Salvation, Others for Damnation? 13

4 Works Don't Matter? 17

5 Under Grace, Not Under the Law? 23

6 Altar Calls and Repentance Are Unnecessary? 29

7 Just an Ole Sinner Saved by Grace? 35

8 The Church Has Replaced Israel? 37

9 Never Mix Faith and Politics? 43

10 The Rapture of the Church? 47

11 Revived Roman Empire and the Pope Is the Antichrist? 53

12 Christians Are Always Healed? 57

13 All Christians Should Be Wealthy? 61

14 More Than One Road Leads to Heaven? 67

15 Universalism—Everyone Is Saved? 71

16 The Gifts of the Spirit Have Ceased? 75

17 Sickness Is a Punishment from God? 79
18 No More Generational Curses? 83
19 All People Are Created in the Image of God? 87
20 We Are All God's Children? 91
21 Never Judge Anybody? 93
22 Hell Means Eternal Suffering for Sinners? 99
23 Satan Is in Charge of Hell? 105
24 Death on the Cross Is the Cruelest Punishment? 107
25 The King James Bible Is the Original Word of God? 111
26 The Scripture Prohibits Female Preachers? 117
27 God Controls Everything on Earth? 121
28 Never Resist the Governing Authorities? 125
29 Jesus Never Claimed to Be God? 131
30 Progressive Christianity? 137
31 Days of Noah or a Huge Spiritual Awakening? 139
Conclusion 145

INTRODUCTION

SEVERAL FALSE TEACHINGS HAVE INFILTRATED OUR CHURCHES today, some of which are extremely dangerous. Spiritual warfare is being waged against societies to capture the souls of nations, to pervert truth, and to weaken the power of the Church. This is not a new phenomenon, however. The apostles of the early Church in the first century also had to deal with this type of spiritual warfare.

The apostles frequently had to confront deceptive teachers who were distorting the truth of the Gospel. So, we shouldn't be surprised by the heresy currently being disseminated in many churches, nor should we be caught off guard by the distortion of truth by ungodly individuals in our culture today.

The absolute truth of God's Word has been under attack almost since the dawn of time. The archenemy of God and of mankind lied to Eve in the Garden of Eden in order to distort the truth, and he's still distorting the truth and deceiving individuals today. There truly is "nothing new under the sun" (Ecclesiastes 1:9).

Many of the false teachings that were unleashed on the early Church are still prevalent in churches today. In churches and throughout our culture, truth is being attacked, distorted, and suppressed to convince people to exchange the truth for a lie. The attack on truth in our culture is so pervasive that many people no longer can discern truth from fiction. Sadly, the distortion of truth also is rife in many of our modern churches today. Ministers who have succumbed to the pressures of political correctness and the social justice agenda are complicit in obscuring the truth and leading gullible people astray.

Unfortunately, many churches have adopted the liberal ideology of our secular society. Pastors leading these churches have failed their congregations miserably. It's unfortunate indeed, but many theologians have yielded to the enticing speech of the evil one. They have allowed themselves to become entangled with the world and have gotten in bed with a very crafty harlot called the *way of death*. Liberal theologians have departed from the path of wisdom and truth and gotten on the road leading to destruction (see Proverbs 7). And they're leading many naïve victims along the same route.

Sincere believers must expose these corrupt ministers and guide nonbelievers to the path of life. In fact, Christians have a responsibility to share the Gospel with others, to expose false theology, and to combat woke ideology to prevent people from falling prey to false teachers and ungodly philosophies. Individuals both within and outside the Church need to be protected from false doctrine and fake theologians that promote damnable lies designed by the wicked one to wreak havoc on societies and steal the souls of men.

Progressive beliefs and woke ideology aren't just running rampant in our culture, but they are making great inroads into churches today. Woke theologians claim that God suddenly has become a progressive who no longer expects people to follow archaic commandments previously established by Him in the Scriptures. The former moral laws of God are now considered old-fashioned and not applicable to our modern society.

In this book, I highlight some of the most widespread false doctrine being taught in churches today and explain how it impacts us and our culture. For example, one false teaching called Gnosticism existed in the first century, but it has reemerged in the modern Church today. This false theology was resurrected several decades ago, and it is now being widely proclaimed in many major denominations.

Gnostic teaching advances the concept that once people accept Christ as their Savior, they're free to live any kind of lifestyle they desire, no matter how ungodly. This doctrine essentially provides people a *sin without remorse* card. According to Gnostic doctrine, there's no need for believers to repent of their sins once they've received Christ as their Savior. Supposedly, the grace of God is boundless and covers all kinds of vile behavior. This is why nonreligious people and those claiming to be Christians often live the same kind of ungodly lifestyles without any guilt or shame whatsoever.

The evil one has convinced many people that God overlooks the most diabolical sins—without any need on the part of believers to repent. The concept is that we have such a kind and merciful God that no more wrath or judgment will be meted out by the Almighty. In biblical times, God the Father was viewed as a stern, judgmental "tough guy"—until Jesus appeared on the scene. Jesus supposedly changed all of that, and now gentle Jesus won't ever judge anybody.

These false concepts of Jesus and sin have led to the preaching of a *feel-good gospel* that never confronts sin, along with an erroneous doctrine known as *eternal security*. This doctrinal belief states that believers remain eternally secure and bound for heaven, even if they later deny the faith and totally reject Christ as Savior.

Another false doctrine that's prevalent in the modern church today is that the Old Testament (OT) is no longer relevant. According to these false teachers, Old Testament Scriptures are outdated, old-fashioned, and just too antiquated to be of any value. OT laws are seen as no longer applicable to our modern culture, because God's ancient laws are too restrictive to apply to the acceptable norms of society today.

Other pagan heresies being promoted in some churches include the idea that multiple roads lead to heaven and that ultimately everybody is saved. The concept that *everybody is saved* envisions an eternity with no punishment for sins and no hell. The belief is: Jesus was punished for the sins of the whole world, so sinners are off the hook—so to speak—and won't be condemned for their unrepentant sins. Further, these false teachers claim that Jesus' sacrifice on the cross also provides many ways in which to reach eternal life. According to them, belief in any god is an acceptable substitute for Jesus as long as individuals are sincere in their faith. This and other cunningly deceptive doctrine is being espoused not only by emergent and progressive churches, but even in some mainline denominations.

Christianity has become so diluted today that large numbers of people don't believe in even the basic tenets of the Christian faith. For many individuals, Jesus has been entirely removed from the equation. Some of the most popular ministers often preach messages that never address sin or convict sinners to repent. These teachers give people goose bumps, make them feel good, and send them home week after week as lost as when they came. None of these churchgoers ever impact the secular community around them for Christ, because they themselves are secular. These folks are counterfeit Christians thinly cloaked in a false religion.

The enemy has used false teachings and a soft-peddled gospel to damage the Church and weaken the faith of many believers. These false beliefs also negatively impact the culture, since the error promoted by the world has infiltrated the Church. It's difficult in many instances to distinguish the worldview of those in church from that of the culture in which they live. Society believes that if churches accept the liberal viewpoints of the culture, then the culture must be right—so there's no need to change the culture! Furthermore, true followers of Christ are perceived as intolerant and bigoted, as people to be avoided and distrusted by the rest of society.

The culture has been instrumental in changing the views and values of the Church, but the Church hasn't had much of an impact in changing the values of the culture. All false theology has been designed by the evil one to damage the effectiveness of the Church and cause prejudicial attitudes toward genuine believers. The wicked one knows that a compromised Church won't be able to fulfill its mission of successfully presenting the Gospel and making disciples of men. False theology is wreaking all kinds of havoc in churches and on secular society as well.

The list of false theological concepts is almost endless, but I have concentrated only on those that are most widely accepted by beleaguered church congregations. This book highlights a number of detrimental and questionable teachings that have been cleverly designed by the devil to undermine the positive influence of the Church in the lives of believers and in the culture at large. Some of the theological concepts are very harmful, while others cause minimal damage to reputation of the Church and to the faith of believers. But none of these theories are without significance.

All false theology should be confronted, challenged, and exposed whenever it's encountered. I heard a kind theologian say recently that he didn't want to slander a false teacher by exposing him. This in itself is wrong theology. This minister has an obligation to expose false teachers, so that gullible people won't be taken captive by false doctrine. Exposing false teachers isn't slander. It's the righteous, just, and kind thing to do. It appears as if the accuser of the brethren has deceived some true ministers of the Gospel into believing that they'll somehow be violating a law of God if they expose evil.

Clearly, it's never wrong to expose the evil of false brethren. Actually, the Bible commands us to expose evil and also to have no fellowship with those who are living ungodly lifestyles (see Ephesians 5:3–7 and 11–12). I believe the "kind" minister who didn't want to be accused of slander actually did his audience a great disservice. There could have been people in his audience who were supporting the false teacher's ministry whom this minister was unwilling to identify.

Many Christians have listened to charismatic preachers and purchased their books to later determine that what they are preaching is false doctrine. I certainly have listened to several theologians whom I later decided were teaching error. These ministers seemed so sincere and their teachings sounded so good initially, until I came to the realization that they were espousing false doctrine.

Be forewarned: Just because something looks good and sounds good, doesn't mean that it is good. The wicked one is very deceptive, and he often disguises false teachers as angels of light. Also, be aware that an establishment with the word *church* included in its name doesn't necessarily mean the institution is a Christian organization. A true Christian church will ordain only moral men or women to preach the Gospel, and godly preachers won't deviate from the teachings of the Bible.

I haven't formatted the false teachings addressed in this book specifically as questions; however, I decided to place a question mark at the end of each theological concept in order to make readers think deeply and question what they believe about these theories.

1

ONCE SAVED, ALWAYS SAVED?

PROBABLY THE WORST AND MOST DAMNABLE RELIGIOUS TEACHING being promoted in the modern Church today is the false Gnostic doctrine of *once saved, always saved,* also known as "eternal security." It's puzzling how intelligent people can embrace this diabolical concept as sound theological doctrine.

This doctrine was not taught in the early Church, but it was taught by heretics in early Church history. The doctrine of *once saved, always saved* was somehow resurrected and currently is going full throttle in many modern churches. In the 1500s, John Calvin reintroduced Gnostic beliefs and began postulating the doctrine of *once saved, always saved.* Regrettably, many ministers and laypersons alike have accepted this false theology today.

One of the most noted pastors today who teaches the damnable doctrine of *once saved, always saved* has a very large congregation in Atlanta, Georgia. Over the many years of his ministry, he undoubtedly has led many gullible, unsuspecting souls astray. I can't imagine a man of his stature and knowledge of the Bible believing and teaching such grievously erroneous theology. I can prove from both the Old Testament and the New Testament Scriptures that this doctrine is unsound.

A number of scriptures from the Old Testament clearly state that righteous people who turn from the way of righteousness will be judged as *sinners* and condemned on the Day of Judgment. Eternal security is guaranteed, but only to those who remain in the faith.

Ezekiel 18:24 states: "But when a righteous man turns away from his righteousness and commits iniquity, and does according to all the abominations that the wicked man does, shall he live? All the righteousness which he has done shall not be remembered; because of the unfaithfulness of which he is guilty and the sin which he has committed, because of them he shall die." Further, Ezekiel 33:18–19 says: "When the righteous turns from his righteousness and commits iniquity, he shall die because of it. But when the wicked turns from his wickedness and does what is lawful and right, he shall live because of it." Once when I quoted these Scriptures to someone, she argued that Ezekiel was referring to physical death. This is nonsense. We will all die physically. These Scriptures clearly are referring to living or dying spiritually.

Likewise, Ezekiel 3:20 and Ezekiel 33:12–13 confirm that righteous people who turn away from the Lord will be condemned and will die spiritually—and their former righteous deeds will not be remembered. Proverbs 21:16 says: "A man who wanders from the way of understanding will rest in the assembly of the dead." Again, this is clearly referring to spiritual death. Furthermore, a person cannot turn away from righteousness or wander from the way of understanding without first being in God's Kingdom. Someone might argue that this is from the time of the Old Testament, before the atonement of Jesus.

Individuals who disdain the Old Testament Scriptures, claiming they are outdated and not relevant today, should respect and be willing to consider what the New Testament Scriptures say about the subject of eternal security. Several New Testament Scriptures indicate that salvation is conditional. Unconditional salvation isn't taught anywhere in the Scriptures.

Salvation is contingent upon individuals remaining in God's grace until they die physically. The apostle Paul taught the Corinthian believers that they were saved—if they *held fast* to the word that he had preached to them; otherwise, they would have believed in vain (see 1 Corinthians 15:1–2). Paul also taught the saints in Colossae that they would be presented holy and blameless to the Lord if they *continued* in the faith and were not moved away from the Gospel of Christ (see Colossians 1:21–23). Hebrews 3:6 states that we are the house of Christ as long as we *hold fast* our confidence (faith) *until the end*. Hebrews 3:14 further indicates: "For we have become partakers of Christ if we *hold* the beginning of our confidence *steadfast to the end*." James, speaking to the twelve tribes of Israel, states in James 5:19–20: "Brethren, if anyone among you wanders from the truth, and someone turns him back, let him know that he who turns a sinner from the error of his way will save a soul from death and cover a multitude of sins."

The apostle Peter says that it would have been better for individuals to never have known Jesus Christ than to have become righteous and then turned away from the truth (see 2 Peter 2:21). Jude calls individuals such as these *twice dead* (Jude 12). Jesus Himself told His disciples in Luke 12:45–46 that believers who question His return and begin to abuse other people will be condemned with sinners. Jesus also indicated in the parable of the prodigal son (Luke 15:11–32) that the prodigal was spiritually dead until he came to his senses and returned to his father. This parable is a picture of a backslidden Christian repenting and coming back into right relationship with his heavenly Father.

Jesus states in the book of Revelation that those who overcome will not be blotted out of the *Book of Life* (Revelation 3:5), which seems to indicate that those who *don't* remain faithful will have their names blotted out. Jesus further states in Revelation 3:15–16 that lukewarm Christians are so repulsive to Him that He will vomit them out of His mouth. The apostle John writes in Revelation 22:18–19 that if anyone adds to or takes away anything from the Word of God, his name will be taken away from the *Book of Life*. Other Scriptures indicating that believers can lose their salvation if they turn away from their righteousness are Hebrews 6:4–6 and Hebrews 10:38–39. Also, read the parables of the wise and foolish virgins in Matthew 25:1–13, the faithful and evil servants in Matthew 24:45–51, and the talents in Matthew 25:14–30.

By the way, theologians who teach the *once saved, always saved* doctrine essentially give people a license to sin. According to them, individuals can live totally immoral lifestyles, never repent, and still be saved and *heaven-ready*. Any logical, rational, godly person should know that this belief grossly violates teachings of the Scriptures.

The apostle Paul explains in Romans 6:1–2 that the grace of God does not give individuals the right to continue in their sin. In fact, Paul is shocked that anyone might promote this doctrine. Paul also advises Timothy how to deal with those who are sinning in the Church. He didn't tell Timothy to ignore sin and not to expose sinful behavior. Instead the apostle Paul states in 1 Timothy 5:20: "Those who are sinning rebuke in the presence of all, that the rest also may fear."

I'm always greatly grieved when former born-again believers depart from the faith and deny Christ. There have been several ministers of the Gospel and worship leaders in recent years who have denied their faith, although I cannot remember any of their names. Several years ago one former Pentecostal preacher–turned comedian–denied his faith and mocked God in his comedy routines. He said diabolical things about God and the Holy Spirit before his death. I don't claim to be the **Salvation Police**, but I believe this former minister of the Gospel likely committed the unpardonable sin of blasphemy against the Holy Spirit (see Matthew 12:31–32; Mark 3:28–29; and Luke 12:10). Individuals who deny Christ after knowing Him insult God the Father, Jesus, and the Holy Spirit. When I hear about these individuals, I feel an almost overwhelming sadness for them.

Some theologians claim that true believers cannot backslide to perdition. They quote John 10:27–29 as justification for their belief.

They indicate that according to these Scriptures and other verses dealing with the issue of salvation that Jesus has given believers eternal life and that no one—not even themselves—is able to remove them from the Father's hand. I, on the other hand, believe these Scriptures must be viewed in proper context with other Scriptures. Yes, Jesus does indeed give us eternal life, and neither the devil nor other people can steal our salvation; however, we all have free will to continue in the faith or to reject Christ.

We, and we alone, have the ability to turn our backs on the Lord Jesus Christ or continue in our faith. Salvation is a free gift from God, and as such we can receive and later reject the gift. Christians can choose to retain the gift to eternal salvation or give the gift back to God. Some individuals say to the Lord, "No, thank You. I've decided it's best for me to go my own way." Shockingly, some people leave their Christian faith in order to follow a false religion. Some individuals blaspheme the Holy Spirit in the process—a sin that can never be forgiven them. Once a person blasphemes the Holy Spirit, there's no path for them back to Jesus.

We cannot offend God and treat Jesus and the blood of Jesus as worthless, and then expect to still be in right standing with God. Likewise, we cannot treat other people badly, be hurtful and unforgiving, and still believe that we are in right relationship with the Lord. We cannot violate the Scriptures in our relationship with people or with God and expect to remain secure in God's Kingdom.

The Bible expresses in numerous Scriptures that some will not inherit the Kingdom of God. Various Scriptures, such as 1 Corinthians 6:9–10, Galatians 5:19–21, and Ephesians 5:5, warn us of the types of individuals who will not make it into heaven.

Salvation and our relationship with Jesus Christ is a bit like a race in an athletic competition. For individuals to win a prize, they must finish the race. If people begin well—but are unable to finish or decide to quit in the middle of the race—they have no chance of winning a prize. This same rule applies to our spiritual race. This is the reason the Lord tells us that we must endure to the end in order to win a crown!

Many believers are just springtime Christians. They're neither hot nor cold. God states in His Word that He won't accept those who are lukewarm. It is of paramount importance that we remain in a right relationship with God the Father, Jesus Christ, and the Holy Spirit. We accomplish this through prayer, worship, repenting, righteous living, loving and forgiving others, and avoiding deceptive teaching that would cause us to cross over from the path of righteousness to the road leading to destruction.

If you've allowed yourself to be deceived by the erroneous unconditional *eternal security* doctrine, I recommend repenting and asking the Holy Spirit to illuminate truth to you. We're cautioned repeatedly throughout the Scriptures not to allow ourselves to become deceived. Believe me, this is something that is very easy to do. The enemy is a master at deception, in getting people to step off the right track and board a train speeding to a different destination. This is a bit like being at a metro station and wandering onto the wrong platform, boarding the wrong train, and ending up at a destination that you never intended. This happened to me once in New York City. When I realized the metro I had taken was going in the wrong direction, I wisely got off at the next stop and boarded a subway car going in the direction of my intended destination.

If this describes your situation, get off the train going in the wrong direction and board the one headed in the right direction. Many people who adhere to the unconditional *eternal security* doctrine are too arrogant to admit that they're imperfect and commit sins like everybody else. Proverbs 28:13 states: "He who covers his sins will not prosper, but whoever confesses and forsakes them will have mercy." Repent and make a course correction is the only advice that the Scriptures and I can offer you.

2

NO NEED TO REPENT AFTER SALVATION—REALLY?

ANOTHER DAMNABLE DOCTRINE THAT IS CLOSELY RELATED TO *once saved, always saved* is the belief that there is no need for people to ever repent of sins they commit after becoming Christians. Some theologians teach that all of our sins have been forgiven (including future sins); therefore, there is no need to ever repent again for wrongdoing or for sins committed after we become born-again believers. Evidently, to them ***salvation means never having to say we're sorry!*** This teaching is a clear violation of Scripture.

The Bible teaches repentance from Genesis to Revelation. Even in the last book of the Bible, Jesus warns believers while addressing the seven churches identified in Revelation of their need to repent. Without repentance, followers of Christ will lose rewards and in some instances even lose their salvation. We are to repent of obvious sins, as well as the hidden sins of the heart.

Jesus gives a stern warning to lukewarm Christians. Clearly, never having to repent after becoming a follower of Christ is a false doctrine. Further, I would warn that it's a very dangerous doctrine that could lead to the loss of a person's entrance into heaven. People cannot be Christians and *heaven-ready* on their own terms; they must follow the standards established by God. In fact, the apostle John warns Christians in 1 John 1:8: "If we say that we have no sin, we deceive ourselves, and the truth is not in us." John further states in 1 John 1:9–10: "If we confess our sins, He is faithful and just to forgive us our sins and to cleanse us from all unrighteousness. If we say that we have not sinned, we make Him a liar, and His word is not in us."

Never having to repent of bad behavior is such an unsound doctrine that I find it mind-boggling that any student of the Bible could buy in to this belief. If people behave badly and offend other individuals, virtually no one in our society would believe that it's acceptable for them not to apologize to the offended parties. If this is true in the natural realm, then it's certainly true in the spiritual realm.

When we behave badly, we should not only ask for forgiveness from those whom we have hurt, but we also must ask God to forgive us. The converse is also true. If someone offends us, we are required to forgive them as well. These beliefs are Theology 101, supported not only by polite society but also by the Word of God.

The Lord requires us to forgive others. Matthew 6:14–15 states: "For if you forgive men their trespasses, your heavenly Father will also forgive you. But if you do not forgive men their trespasses, neither will your Father forgive your trespasses." Mark 11, verses

25–26, tell us that if we are praying and remember that someone has offended us, we are to forgive them prior to continuing our prayers. If we choose not to forgive them, neither will the Lord forgive our sins. If we don't forgive other people, this means that we have unforgiven sins piling up in our spiritual account!

Read the parable of the unforgiving servant in Matthew 18:21–35. Clearly, we are to forgive others in order to be forgiven by God. Forgiving other people is exhibiting godly behavior—showing love, mercy, and kindness—as our Lord has shown and continues to show to us.

All the discord and black-versus-white rage in our culture is simply a ploy of the devil to steal people's souls. The scheme of the enemy is to cause people to feel hatred toward each other and to harbor unforgiveness toward other people. But the Bible is clear that entrance into God's Kingdom requires people to love one another and to forgive others. All of us fail greatly, but it should be our goal to show love, kindness, and forgiveness toward other people—even toward those with whom we disagree. We must be quick to forgive, to ask for forgiveness from others and from God, and to repent.

If individuals think logically about the idea of **"never having to say they're sorry,"** they cannot possibly come to any other conclusion except that this doesn't make sense when applied to the Almighty. If a person says or does anything that harms another individual, they are expected to apologize to the person whom they have injured. If this concept applies in most cultures—and we need to ask individuals to forgive us for hurting them—how can this not also apply in our relationship with God?

I am absolutely confounded by the number of individuals who find no need to repent of bad behavior, and the numerous

Christians who continue to harbor unforgiveness in their hearts. The Bible tells us that people such as these are in danger of hellfire. Yet, these folks continue in their sins completely without remorse, and seemingly without an awareness of any danger. Unforgiving people have a very serious heart issue that will ban them from heaven—unless they repent.

The Scriptures instruct us to guard our hearts. We also must frequently ask the Lord to search our hearts in order to ensure we're still living pure lives. We cannot rely wholly on our own hearts to keep us from error and protect us from deception and sin. It's very easy for people who walk in the flesh, rather than the Spirit, to deceive themselves—especially concerning their relationship with Christ and about their non-Christian attitudes toward other people. This is particularly true in churches where pastors concentrate too heavily on grace and ignore the importance of repenting of sins and living in the Spirit.

We are cautioned by the Word of God not to trust too heavily in our own hearts to lead us. The Bible warns that our hearts can be deceptive, even desperately wicked (see Jeremiah 17:9). Also, Proverbs 28:26 says: "He who trusts in his own heart is a fool, but whoever walks wisely will be delivered."

We are admonished numerous times in the Scriptures not to allow ourselves to be deceived. We walk wisely when we don't allow our own hearts to deceive us, and when we don't allow ourselves to be deceived by other people. Believing that it's unnecessary to repent is a deceptive doctrine designed by the evil one to weaken or destroy a person's faith, and perhaps ultimately to steal an individual's salvation.

3

GOD CHOOSES SOME FOR SALVATION, OTHERS FOR DAMNATION?

YET ANOTHER FALSE DOCTRINE THAT'S CLOSELY RELATED TO *once saved, always saved* is the religious belief that some people are created by God for salvation, while others have been created specifically for damnation. John Calvin is credited as the author of this false doctrine known as Calvinism. This doctrine is clearly wrong and is based on a few verses of Scripture that have been misinterpreted and taken out of context. The Bible clearly states that God desires for *all* people to be saved and come to the knowledge of the truth (see 1 Timothy 2:4 and 2 Peter 3:9).

According to the Word of God, the Lord takes no pleasure in the death of wicked people, but He does take pleasure in the death of His saints (see Ezekiel 33:11 and Psalm 116:15). God knows that wrath and destruction await unrepentant sinners, while eternal life is secured for those followers of Christ who remain faithful to the end. Christians will enjoy being sons and daughters of God and living in His presence forever! Calvinism is particularly disturbing because it discourages some individuals from seeking salvation, because they believe they were born for damnation. On the other hand, Calvinism causes other people to believe that they can live ungodly lifestyles and still be saved, since they are apparently God's chosen *elect.*

Two of the worst beliefs associated with Calvinism are known as predestination (unconditional election) and the perseverance of the saints (unconditional eternal security). Calvinists believe that some individuals are predestined by God for salvation (heaven), while others are predestined for condemnation (hell). The predestined (chosen) individuals are known as the *elect,* and salvation is absolutely guaranteed to these individuals. Calvinism states that since these people are chosen by God to be saved, they will **definitely be saved.** In other words, at some point in their lives, the grace of God will overwhelm them and can no longer be resisted by those chosen for salvation; they *certainly* will be saved *period.* The chosen *elect* not only cannot resist God's grace forever, but they are eternally secure—and they cannot ever fall from God's grace. The unconditional eternal security portion of Calvinism has been adopted by several mainline denominations today.

Another belief that Calvinists hold is that of limited atonement—the sacrifice of Jesus on the cross was limited to the *chosen elect* only—and everybody else is just totally out of luck. This concept is that those individuals who are not included in the limited atonement of Christ cannot ever be saved, even if they desperately want to know Jesus.

Although I don't agree with Calvinist doctrine, I believe some people adhering to this doctrine may be sincere followers of Christ. They simply are condoning very flawed doctrine based on Scriptures that have been interpreted out of context. By exposing false doctrine, I am not necessarily exposing false teachers or even counterfeit Christians. Individuals can believe erroneous doctrine without being condemned, as long as they adhere to the major foundational principles of the Christian faith—the virgin birth, crucifixion and resurrection of Jesus, sacrificial atonement, repentance and justification, salvation by grace, and the belief that Jesus is the only way to the Father and eternal life. Probably none of us believe absolutely perfectly, but we should study the Word of God and ask the Lord to illuminate the Scriptures to us.

4

WORKS DON'T MATTER?

SOME THEOLOGIANS TEACH THAT WE ARE SAVED BY GRACE ALONE; therefore, works are unimportant. This teaching is only partially biblical. It's true that we are saved by grace through our faith in Christ. It is also true, however, that genuine salvation will be accompanied by godly works. The Bible tells us that Abraham believed God, and it was credited to him as righteousness (see Genesis 15:6; Romans 4:3; and James 2:23–24). Abraham believed God, but he proved it by his actions and obedience. Abraham obeyed God, and he lived to please Him.

Like Abraham, we must live our lives in obedience to God. Individuals who accept Jesus as their Savior cannot continue to live any way they like, ignoring the boundaries established by God's standards. It's true that we are saved by grace and not by good works. But it's also true that we are saved by faith combined with good works and obedience. If there is no moral change or no righteous deeds once sinners pray the prayer of salvation, then the sinners most likely did not get legitimately saved.

Praying what is known as the *sinner's prayer* doesn't save anyone. For a person to be authentically saved and become a born-again follower of Jesus Christ, that individual must show works of repentance. If there is no noticeable change in an individual's behavior and lifestyle, then the salvation isn't genuine—and that individual is still lost in his or her sins.

The Bible cautions us in Philippians 2:12 that we are to work out our own salvation with fear and trembling. This doesn't mean that we are to strive for our salvation, but rather that we are to ensure that we are legitimately saved. If we are sensitive to the Holy Spirt, the Lord will reveal our spiritual condition to us. Romans 8:16 assures us with these words: "The Spirit Himself bears witness with our spirit that we are children of God."

We are saved by grace, but we are kept in God's Kingdom by continuing in that grace by faith and accomplishing the good works He has prepared for us to do. A lot of ministers of the Gospel today preach hyper-grace, but the Bible tells us that we're to be doers of the law and not hearers only (see Romans 2:13).

Certainly, grace and faith are of paramount importance, but good works are necessary as well. Ephesians 2:8–9 reads: "For by grace you have been saved through faith, and that not of yourselves; it is the gift of God, not of works, lest anyone should boast." Most people stop reading their Bibles at these verses. But the apostle Paul continues his teaching to the Ephesian believers in Ephesians 2:10, which says: "For we are His workmanship, created in Christ Jesus for good works, which God prepared beforehand that we should walk in them." This is the rest of the story!

Clearly, we are saved by grace through believing—having faith. Salvation is a free gift from God when we repent and believe in Jesus. This means believing the Word of God, from the book of Genesis through the book of Revelation. This means that we believe in the life, death, and resurrection of Jesus Christ, and in the atonement provided for us by Jesus' death on the cross and His resurrection. Once we receive this wonderful free gift provided to us by the sacrifice of Jesus, we are expected to live a life pleasing to God. We also are expected to bring glory to our heavenly Father by the good deeds we do in compliance with His will.

We cannot continue to live a life of habitual sin and be true disciples of Jesus Christ. Our speech and behavior will reflect whether we are true believers or just counterfeit Christians. Again, we cannot live just *any ole way* we want. Our lifestyle and deeds must show that we have become new creations in Christ Jesus. Our deeds or works will confirm what type of people we truly are.

The apostle James tells us that faith without works is dead (see James 2:17). James further states that the faith of Christians will be shown by their works. James 2:18 says: "Show me your faith without your works, and I will show you my faith by my works." Faith is not true faith without corresponding works. Faith isn't just a mental assent only. Good works reflect faith; a believer's faith is made evident by works or actions. James 2:22 indicates that Abraham's faith was made perfect by his works.

Many times there are deathbed conversions where new believers won't be able to show their faith by their works. These cases, however, are exceptions. I'm personally suspicious of many deathbed conversions to Christ. I know they happen, and many of these sinners are genuinely saved. At the same time, I also believe that some deathbed conversions aren't authentic—and these individuals die in their sins. Anyone can repeat the *sinner's prayer*. Just repeating a prayer, without faith, doesn't justify or convert anyone to Christ.

The Bible tells us that without faith it is impossible to please God (see Hebrews 11:6). Faith is the first order of business with God, because without faith we can't please Him. Without faith, we cannot be saved. Without faith, we cannot truly love God and genuinely love others. Without faith, we cannot be healed. Without faith, we cannot do the good, godly deeds the Lord has prepared for us to accomplish. So you can see how grace and faith work hand in hand to help us do good works. Grace is just one part of the equation. Faith must be present to receive grace, and faith must work with grace in order to accomplish good deeds for the glory of God.

The bottom line is that grace and our good deeds work together! If we have received the grace of God to salvation, we will have good deeds (works) that glorify God. At the same time, no one can work their way into heaven. Many false religions teach working one's way into God's Kingdom, but they fail to teach faith in Jesus Christ. Without the Lord's blessing on our works, then our works and righteous acts are seen by God as nothing but filthy rags (see Isaiah 64:6).

Virtually all false religions require working one's way into heaven, which cannot be done. False religions reduce Jesus to a *tiny* god, while elevating deeds (filthy rags) to the heights of heaven. Filthy rags or serving a Jesus other than the One who died on the cross for our sins is futile. Individuals must receive the resurrected Christ of the Holy Bible; otherwise, they are still in their sins—and their good works will be rejected by God and will profit them nothing.

Good deeds of unbelievers or those accomplished with wrong motives are counted as worthless before God. For believers, good works matter, and they matter a lot! James 1:22 says: "But be doers of the word, and not hearers only, deceiving yourselves." In addition, we are told in James 2:24 that a man is justified by works, and not by faith alone. Further, James 2:26 states: "For as the body without the spirit is dead, so faith without works is dead also." So, you see, salvation is granted by the grace of God through faith, but our faith is kept solid and unshakeable by following the Word of God and by accomplishing good works. Do not be deceived—your works matter to God!

Works and good deeds are the basis for receiving rewards in heaven. Worthless deeds, those done without proper motives, will be judged by God and burned up. Only righteous deeds, approved by God, will remain and will receive rewards (see 1 Corinthians 3:14–15).

5

UNDER GRACE, NOT UNDER THE LAW?

Many theologians teach that Christians are no longer under the Law, but are under grace. And many individuals extend this doctrine to mean that the Ten Commandments are no longer applicable. Therefore, they can live any kind of lifestyle they desire and still inherit the Kingdom of heaven. But what does it really mean to be under grace and not under the Law?

Well, first of all, the moral laws are still in effect. Hopefully, no one believes that the grace of God gives us permission to murder, rape, maim, steal, commit adultery, lie, defile the Sabbath, dishonor our parents, worship idols, disrespect God, and break all the other moral laws of God. We still should be obeying the standards that God set forth in the Ten Commandments and in other Scriptures contained in the New Testament.

Ungodly people oppose the standards of God and have tried to dismiss the Ten Commandments as no longer relevant to our society today. They also oppose other moral laws, not specifically contained in the Ten Commandments, such as laws relating to marriage and sexual purity. Many people today would even argue that the command not to murder doesn't apply to unborn babies, and that lying doesn't apply to politicians or journalists. Without any shame whatsoever, many people openly embrace abortion, lying, stealing, and committing adultery.

Virtually anything goes nowadays—stealing elections, ruining a person's reputation, murdering babies at the time of birth and calling it abortion, same-sex marriage, changing one's gender (in reality not even medically or biologically possible), sex trafficking, violently destroying cities during *so-called peaceful* protests, and many other gross sins.

The lifestyles of many people today are so outside the realm of God's standards that even individuals claiming to be Christians call evil things good. Isaiah 5:20 states: "Woe to those who call evil good, and good evil; who substitute darkness for light and light for darkness; who substitute bitter for sweet, and sweet for bitter!" (NASB). This attitude is prevalent throughout our country and in societies around the world. In fact, this attitude is so widespread that many people can no longer distinguish between good and evil. They have reprobate minds; their consciences have been seared, making it almost impossible for them to discern the truth (see Romans 1:28 and 1 Timothy 4:2).

People's behavior and conversations have become totally uncivil toward each other. But people everywhere should heed the warning contained in Matthew 12:37, which says: "For by your words you will be justified, and by your words you will be condemned." Individuals also should carefully consider 2 Corinthians 5:10, which states: "For we must all appear before the judgment seat of Christ, that each one may receive the things done in the body, according to what he has done, whether good or bad."

Some misguided theologians who may be well-meaning have misinterpreted the Scriptures to suggest principles that God never intended. Their teaching about grace so seriously violates the Scriptures that it is dangerous and can only be called what it is—false doctrine. Any doctrine indicating that believers are no longer subject to the moral laws of God is shockingly deficient.

We are no longer under the curse of the Law, which means that we no longer have to sacrifice animals to cover our sins. Jesus paid the price for our sins on the cross. He died on the cross, so we don't have to kill and sacrifice the blood of animals when we sin. All we have to do is repent of our sins and accept His sacrifice. Jesus died to set us free from the curse of the Law—the curse of offering animal sacrifices for sins. Although the sacrifice of Jesus did away with the curse of the Law, it didn't abolish the moral part of the Law. Jesus came to fulfill the Law, not to abolish it (Matthew 5:17).

New Testament laws actually are even stricter than those contained in the Old Testament. In the Old Testament, a person had to physically kill someone in order to be guilty of murder, but under New Testament law, anyone who hates his brother is guilty of committing murder. An individual in Old Testament times had to physically commit adultery, but in New Testament times, a person only has to look at another individual with sexual lust in order to commit adultery. So you can see how the laws have become much stricter and more difficult to obey today than in Old Testament times. We won't be judged just for our actions, but also for the intent and motives of our hearts that only God can discern.

God looks at the motives of our hearts, not just our outward actions. Many individuals read this in their Bibles, but they don't seem to understand this concept—nor do they fully understand law and grace. So theologians often teach a grace message that's so badly flawed that it truly doesn't describe grace at all. This means that many rules are tossed out in order to embrace more modern thinking. Yet, where rules or boundaries established by the Lord are abandoned, disorder ensues.

Crime and immorality are bad enough in the world without God's standards being violated in churches as well. I don't think it is a coincidence that so much sin and violence take place on the weekend, which includes the Sabbath. People in many cities begin their reign of terror on Friday evening and continue until Monday morning. In several violent cities, there are multiple shootings and several murders every single weekend. Many cities are almost overwhelmed by violence, drunkenness, and wild partying. Mayhem results when the boundaries God has set for humanity are violated.

Rules and boundaries were established by God to protect us from ourselves and from other people. Without moral laws, humanity would live totally immoral lives, and the whole earth would be corrupted, just like in the days of Noah. Our entire society and the whole of the earth would become a cesspool. We are almost there now!

Again, the moral laws still apply to society today, whether people like the rules or not. Only the sacrificial laws were done away with when Jesus died on the cross for our sins. Also, we aren't required to keep the commandments perfectly, which no one can do anyway. Unfortunately, Jewish religious leaders added many additional laws that Jews still try to obey today. I once heard a story about a Jewish woman in Israel who was piously observing the Sabbath. She was staying at the same hotel as a tour group from the United States. She approached one of the American tourists and asked if a woman would be kind enough to help her. The American lady was willing to help and asked the Jewish woman what she needed, at which point the Jewish lady explained that she needed help turning on the light switch in her hotel room. The Jewish woman had forgotten to flip on a light switch before leaving the hotel earlier in the day. When she returned to her room, it was dark. Since it was the Sabbath, the Jewish lady wasn't allowed to turn on a light switch without violating the Sabbath! The simple task of turning on a light was considered work on the Sabbath—a serious violation of the commandment not to work on the Sabbath. Now, that's bondage!

God never intended for any of us to live in that kind of bondage, while trying to honor the Sabbath. Second Corinthians 3:6 states: "For the letter kills, but the Spirit gives life." The Jewish woman who was trying to follow the letter of the law most likely was reading the Torah *only,* and she had no idea that she could be set free by the blood of Jesus. She simply didn't understand the grace of God. Not unlike Jewish religious leaders whom have imposed legalistic rules on individuals, some Christian pastors also teach a legalistic faith. They have constructed their own "*do* and *don't do*" lists. Trying to keep manmade rules violates the Scriptures. No one can perfectly obey the Law, nor can anyone be justified by following a list of rules. At the same time, we must not throw out God's standards and create our own standards of morality and holiness.

There is error on both sides of the fence! On one side, hyper-grace allows people so much freedom that they can do virtually anything without falling out of a right relationship with God. On the other side of the fence, legalism doesn't allow even an *imagined* minor infraction of the Law without causing God to disown people.

Hyper-grace was refuted by the apostles in the early Church. Although legalism existed among the religious leaders at the time of Christ, the apostle Paul later took the Galatians to task for practicing legalism. Both hyper-grace and legalism still exist and are practiced in many churches today. Both are wrong theology!

Individuals on both sides of the fence need to study the Scriptures, pray for wisdom, and ensure that they truly know the Lord Jesus Christ as their Savior. Jesus freed people from the heavy burden of legalistic religion, but He didn't free folks to live ungodly lifestyles.

Hyper-grace isn't authentic grace; it is false grace and a false gospel. Nobody should trust in a hyper type of grace, without attending to other weighty matters of the Law, such as justice, mercy, love, and faith. The apostle Paul warned believers in 1 Corinthians, chapter 10, to obey the commandments of God, and not to follow the evil conduct displayed by the Israelites in the Old Testament. Paul indicated that Israel's disobedience and spiritual mistakes were included in the Bible for our benefit—as examples for us and for our admonishment. Clearly, the Scriptures show us commandments and laws that we should obey and sins that we should avoid in order to please God and honor Jesus.

6

ALTAR CALLS AND REPENTANCE ARE UNNECESSARY?

YET ANOTHER DOCTRINE WITHOUT A SYLLABLE OF BIBLICAL authority or truth in it is that altar calls aren't necessary because most people can be saved by osmosis. In other words, the good deeds of a local church will suddenly make people realize their need for salvation. The concept is that individuals who are recipients of charity from churches in their communities will automatically choose to accept Jesus Christ as their Savior without any other intervention on the part of Christians.

Pastors leading these "social justice" churches don't believe in teaching about repentance lest they offend sinners, nor do they hold altar calls to encourage sinners to accept Jesus as their Savior. These misguided ministers also frequently don't teach the Gospel;

they simply give people a "pep talk" or discuss social issues without providing the true answer to life's problems. Jesus is the solution to all societal issues. Romans 10:14 says: "How then shall they call on Him in whom they have not believed? And how shall they believe in Him of whom they have not heard? And how shall they hear without a preacher?" Further, Roman 10:15 indicates that individuals can only preach the Gospel if they have been sent. That is the problem with churches nowadays: Many theologians have **NOT** been sent! Many theologians have sent themselves; they haven't been sent by God.

As I stated earlier, salvation through osmosis is not a scriptural concept. Most people don't accept Jesus on their own initiative just by acknowledging the good deeds of Christians. It is true that some individuals read the Bible, understand what they have read, repent of their sins, and accept Jesus as their Savior of their own volition—but this is the exception rather than the rule. Clearly, these individuals have heard the Gospel before and are motivated by the Holy Spirit to read the Bible and receive Christ, but this is extremely rare. Most osmosis conversions never happen!

Another concept that is closely related to salvation by osmosis is salvation without repentance. Some pastors hold altar calls in which they ask individuals desiring to know Jesus to repeat a salvation prayer after them. This commonly known *sinner's prayer* often is no more than a ritual. Frequently these prayers never even mention repentance.

The *sinner's prayer* is often a benign prayer that doesn't require repentance or any commitment on the part of the sinners. More often than not, individuals come to church as sinners and leave as sinners. But these individuals are usually told that they are born-again believers; they are to attend church; they should read their Bibles; and they can then "go forth and prosper." In other words, *may the force be with them* and may they return again to digest more non-repentance teachings! This is the reason so many individuals sitting in churches week after week are not true followers of Christ and have absolutely no hope of attaining heaven. They have a false sense of security, as do many of those individuals who accept the false doctrine of unconditional eternal security. Eternal life is guaranteed, but it's conditional!

As I stated previously, I'm not the **Salvation Police**, but I believe many people claiming to be followers of Christ are counterfeit Christians. Some of them know they're fakers, while others sincerely believe they are authentic Christians. Often we are too eager and quick to declare someone a believer who has prayed the *sinner's prayer.* If individuals have no heart change, no behavioral change, and no noticeable change in their lifestyle after confessing Christ, then they most likely aren't the real deal. Repeating a prayer and showing no change in one's behavior indicates that they didn't actually understand the Gospel message, didn't truly repent, and didn't accept Jesus Christ as their Lord and Savior.

While altar calls aren't mentioned in the Scriptures, they certainly serve a purpose today, especially in megachurches where there is very little human contact with the individuals sitting in the services. Altar calls are also vital when holding large crusades with thousands of people in attendance.

Altar workers need to be properly trained, however, to ensure that the people coming forward to receive Jesus as their Savior actually understand the Gospel and their need to repent and to be born again. The audiences generally were much smaller in the early Church, so there was more individual contact with the people listening to the apostles and disciples who were ministering the Gospel. House churches often were the norm, and people knew each other intimately. This made it easier and more comfortable for individuals to ask for and receive prayer for salvation and for other spiritual or physical needs.

Altar calls today can be very beneficial for ministering to the spiritual and physical needs of saints and for leading new believers to faith in Christ. We should share the Gospel and help those in need, but we should never try to pressure people into believing. Jesus never tried to force sinners to believe in Him—He never tried to forcefully persuade them to accept Him. Jesus deeply cared about Israel and all people, but He didn't force Himself on anyone. He asked His disciples to go into all the world and preach the Gospel (Matthew 28:19–20 and Mark 16:15), but if people wouldn't receive the Gospel, the disciples were told to shake the dust off their feet and move on to other folks (see Matthew 10:14; Mark 6:11; and Luke 9:5).

We should minister to those in need but not waste our time sharing the Gospel with individuals who have no interest in salvation. At the same time, we shouldn't pass up golden opportunities to share the Gospel with folks who inquire or show an interest. But we must not try to force-feed sinners; only share the Gospel with people who are willing to listen. Those who believe, repent, and are baptized will be saved (Mark 16:16 and John 3:3).

Some ministers don't ask sinners to openly repent of their sins, because they don't want to embarrass them in front of the church congregation. But this is not scriptural. Matthew 10:32–33, Mark 8:38, and Luke 12:8–9 indicate that anyone who is ashamed of Christ will be denied by Jesus before His Father in heaven, and anyone not ashamed of Jesus will be accepted. Matthew 10:32–33 says: "Therefore whoever confesses Me before men, him I will also confess before My Father who is in heaven. But whoever denies Me before men, him I will also deny before My Father who is in heaven."

I would be the first to admit that it does seem a bit intimidating to walk forward to an altar and confess that you're a sinner in front of an entire church congregation. But it's the right thing to do! It is the devil who tries to embarrass individuals and keep them from openly confessing that they're sinners in need of the Savior—Jesus Christ.

I believe sinners can be sincerely saved without responding to an altar call. Some people initially may be embarrassed and may choose to repent of their sins while seated with the church audience, or they may repent later at home. This doesn't mean these individuals aren't legitimately saved; however, it's a good idea for them to confess their faith openly and quickly to other people. This helps to solidify their faith and will make them more conscious of their relationship with Christ. This also will close an avenue from which the devil may try to accuse them of not being legitimate believers. Christians are to confess and profess their faith openly. There are no "secret believers."

7

JUST AN OLE SINNER SAVED BY GRACE?

SOME CHURCHES TEACH THAT THEIR CONVERTS TO CHRISTIANITY are just ole sinners saved by grace. Theologians leading these churches often state that they are simply wretched sinners who just happen to have been saved by the grace of their Lord Jesus Christ. This concept is not biblical.

Once individuals are born-again believers, they become new creations in Christ Jesus. They're no longer "ole sinners"; they are saints and children of God. People are unwise to accept this false theology. If individuals believe they are "ole sinners," not new creations who have become sons and daughters of God, what is to prevent them from behaving like sinners, not saints? This doctrine is a gross misunderstanding of the Word of God. It also encourages believers to remain children, rather than mature into sons of God.

We would be wise to heed the warning in Galatians 4:1, which states: "Now I say that the heir, as long as he is a child, does not differ at all from a slave, though he is master of all." The Bible clearly tells Christians that they are no longer sinners once they accept Jesus as their Savior. Second Corinthians 5:17 states: "Therefore, if anyone is in Christ, he is a new creation; old things have passed away; behold, all things have become new."

The "ole sinner" and the sinful nature pass away when a person becomes a follower of Christ, and the person is re-created in God's righteous image. This does not mean that Christians will always exhibit perfect behavior and never sin, but a true follower of Christ will not continue to live an ungodly lifestyle. They also will be quick to repent and make things right with God, and with others as necessary. Godly behavior identifies true Christians from obnoxious pretenders.

The Bible tells us in Matthew 7:20 that the type of person an individual truly is can be identified by that person's fruits (actions). Wicked individuals often claim to be Christians, but their behavior betrays them. These people are easy to identify, because of the immoral lifestyles they lead. They often violate virtually every commandment of God. No one who is a true follower of Christ will continue to live a habitual life of sin. And true followers of Jesus should never be referred to as *ole sinners,* but rather saints as of the Most High God.

8

THE CHURCH HAS REPLACED ISRAEL?

MANY THEOLOGIANS TEACH THAT THE CHRISTIAN CHURCH HAS replaced Israel as God's chosen people, but the Scriptures do not teach this concept—nor did the early Church teach this theology. This false doctrine is known as ***replacement theology***.

I suppose most, if not all, Christians have heard the theory that the modern Church has replaced the Jews as God's chosen people due to Israel's unbelief and rejection of Jesus Christ. Replacement theology promotes the concept that because the majority of the Jews rejected Jesus as their Messiah, God rejected them and gave their covenant and their promises to the Christian Church instead. In other words, the modern Church—largely made up of Gentiles—has replaced Israel and the Jewish people as God's chosen people. This simply isn't true! There is not a single verse of Scripture that postulates this doctrine, but this bad theology dominated Church history for almost 1,800 years, from the second century AD until the twentieth century. In fact, this theology continues to be taught in some churches today. This is a serious issue, as bad theology usually results in bad behavior, even cruel behavior.

This particular theology has resulted in rabid anti-Semitism among Christians. For centuries, people in general, and Christians in particular, saw the Jewish people as contemptible "Christ killers" who deserved to suffer atrocities. Many people believed the Jews should be brutally punished for killing the Messiah. Both Christians and nonbelievers were responsible for mercilessly persecuting God's chosen people—people whom God repeatedly assured in the Scriptures that He would never leave nor totally forsake. Yet these Scriptures were willfully ignored by diabolical people throughout the centuries in order to maliciously mistreat and exterminate millions of Jewish people.

In the first century AD, Jews were persecuted and often killed for their faith. The persecution of Jewish people has continued throughout history. In 325 AD, the Council of Nicaea branded Jews as diabolical people. In the sixth century AD, Jews were forbidden from holding public office anywhere in Europe. In the eleventh century AD, the Crusaders massacred tens of thousands of Jews supposedly for the sake of Christ. In the thirteenth century AD, all Jews were expelled from England. In the fourteenth century AD, all Jews were forced out of France. Then in 1492, thousands of Jews were killed in Spain during the Inquisition, and those who survived were driven out of the country. From 1215 AD to 1944 AD, various councils enacted laws requiring Jews to wear distinguishing clothing and reside in ghettoes, separated from Christian society. Jews were forced to wear colored badges, hats, armbands, and other clothing in order to distinguish them and set them apart from the rest of society. And of course, the Holocaust resulted in the deaths of millions of Jews throughout Europe, one of the greatest atrocities man has perpetrated against man.

In spite of the cruelty and crimes exacted against the Israelites, the Jews still managed to survive for many centuries without a homeland. Their homeland was reestablished in 1948, when Israel became an independent nation. The Hebrew language also had completely died out and was revived. When the Jewish people declared their independence and their land was established as the modern State of Israel in 1948, five Arab nations (Egypt, Iraq, Syria, Jordan, and Lebanon) declared war on this new country. The total population of Israel at that time, including foreigners, was well under one million people. The total population of their enemies was over twenty-eight million people. Yet, as impossible as it seemed at the time, Israel won the war!

During that period of history, the Jewish State of Israel was populated with poor people who formally had lived in ghettoes and who had previously had their property and financial resources confiscated. Almighty God obviously fought for them, for their independence, and for their survival in 1948; and He will do it again. At the end of the age, Jesus will return to Jerusalem, and He has promised to fight a final battle against the enemies of Israel (Zechariah 14:3).

Numerous Scriptures declare God's loyalty to the Jewish people and to the nation of Israel. Deuteronomy 14:2 declares: "For you are a holy people to the LORD your God, and the LORD has chosen you to be a people for Himself, a special treasure above all the peoples who are on the face of the earth." The apostle Paul announces in Romans 11 that God has not forsaken or cast away His people (the Jews). Romans 11 states unequivocally that Israel has not rejected God forever, nor has God rejected the Jewish people forever. There are numerous Scriptures throughout the Bible that indicate the Lord will not leave or forsake His people Israel, nor will He break the covenant that He made with them through Abraham.

God refers to His people Israel as a special possession and His inheritance; the covenant He made with Israel is secure. The covenant that the Lord made with the Jews through Abraham was unconditional. So, God has not reneged on His promise to the Israelites and now given their covenant to the Gentiles, as some theologians falsely proclaim. The apostle Paul clarifies the position of God concerning Gentiles and His covenant with Israel in Romans 11. Paul explains how God extends His grace to the Gentiles while keeping His covenant firm with Israel.

Replacement theology has been responsible for anti-Semitic attitudes and violence against Jewish people for many centuries. Jews have been discriminated against and treated as "Christ killers" by many people. Misguided individuals evidently have misinterpreted Acts 4:10, Acts 5:30, and Acts 7:52, where the disciples confronted the religious leaders of their day, accusing them of crucifying and murdering Jesus. While it's true that the religious leaders of Jesus' day were partially responsible for killing Jesus, we are all guilty of the crucifixion of Christ. He died for all of our sins, so in a very real sense, all of us participated in the crucifixion of Jesus!

The misinterpretation of some Scriptures in the book of Acts has led to Jewish people being vilified, hated, and mistreated literally for centuries. In fact, anti-Semitic attitudes still exist today. But clearly, God has not rejected the Jews, and His unconditional covenant with Abraham still stands. The Lord indicated that He would bless the Jewish people and all the peoples of the earth through His servant Abraham. The devil has tried to derail God's covenant with Abraham by trying to destroy the Jewish people.

In past centuries, Jewish people were seen as inferior to other races, largely due to misquoted Scriptures in the Bible. This is the reason that they fell victim to the madness of Hitler and were killed in massive numbers during the Holocaust. Again, because of such bad theology concerning Jewish people, they were expelled from many countries, brutalized by angry people, exterminated by demented madmen, had their property stolen, were forced to live in ghettoes, and have suffered more racial discrimination than any other group of people on the planet. Satan is the author of all of these diabolical deeds, carried out by evil people against the Jews. The Holocaust and mass grave sites attest to these truths. People who deny these facts are dishonest individuals, diabolical liars, and criminally insane.

Further, those teaching that the modern Church has replaced the Jews as God's chosen people are greatly deceived and are being used as mouthpieces of the wicked one. Both the Old and New Testaments make it clear that God will gather His people (Israel) and will fight for them against other nations who try to destroy them at the end of the age. Israel is the apple of God's eye, and Jerusalem is the city of God. Also, a special blessing is promised to any individual (or nation) that honors the Jewish people or who prays for the peace of Jerusalem (see Psalm 122:6–7). Also, Genesis 12:3 indicates that those who bless the Jewish people will be blessed and those who curse the nation of Israel will be cursed.

Many Scriptures refute the false claim that God has rejected the Jewish people and has replaced them with the Christian Church (see Deuteronomy 7:6–8; 2 Samuel 7:24; 1 Kings 8:53; 1 Chronicles 17:22; 2 Chronicles 9:8; Psalm 94:14; Psalm 105:8–15; Isaiah 41:8; Isaiah 44:21; Jeremiah 31:1–34; Ezekiel 36:24–28; Ezekiel 37:21–28; Joel 3:2; and Hebrews 8:8–12).

9

NEVER MIX FAITH AND POLITICS?

ANOTHER ERRONEOUS TEACHING IS THAT FAITH AND POLITICS shouldn't mix, because faith is spiritual, and politics is secular. Therefore, it's acceptable and even encouraged by some for Christians to sever their faith from their political views. Christians are being taught by savvy politicians and corrupt theologians that it's okay, and perhaps even desirable, to vote for liberal politicians whose policies violate the standards of their Christian faith. But why is this being taught? There is much personal gain (power and prestige) for dishonest politicians who are catapulted into office by deceived and naïve people. Also, there are temporary rewards for ministers who are afraid to confront sin.

When pastors or televangelists are aware that much of their congregation or TV-viewing audience are Democrats, they are reluctant to say anything that might offend their audiences. They fear losing financial resources from congregants or donors. It's much easier for pastors and televangelists to say nothing or even encourage people to "vote their conscience," but they never address what voting one's conscience really means. They never expose radical politicians and the dangers they pose to our country, our Christian faith, religious liberty, and Christian values.

The Lord gave me a vision in 2020 of Christians whose hands were literally dripping with the blood of aborted babies—based on their voting records for ungodly candidates who hold radical worldviews. Many Democrat politicians, in particular, promote late-term abortion (infanticide) and other ungodly laws that Christians should take no part in helping to enact. Policies of radical Democrats and liberal Republicans are in direct opposition to biblical values and in violation of the Word of God. Christians must realize that everything they do in life is spiritual, and they must stop seeing some things as "secular" and other things as "spiritual."

Believers are not to love the world and the things of the world, nor are they to be unequally yoked with unbelievers (see James 4:4 and 1 John 2:15–16). In fact, these Scriptures indicate that if we love the world and are friends with the world, we are enemies of God, and the love of the Father is not in us. Second Corinthians 6:14 states: "Do not be unequally yoked together with unbelievers. For what fellowship has righteousness with lawlessness? And what communion has light with darkness?"

Christians should not be yoked up with ungodly politicians, false teachers of the Gospel, or other ungodly people. We are to share the message of Jesus with sinners, but we aren't to hang out with them routinely and approve of their lifestyles. And we certainly aren't to participate in enacting ungodly laws that will negatively impact our culture for generations to come. I simply cannot understand how people claiming to be Christians are unable to grasp this concept.

It seems impossible that any true follower of Christ would knowingly vote for a politician with a radical worldview. It's unconscionable that any person claiming to be a Christian would continue to support the platform of the Democratic National Committee. The radical agenda of Democrats should be abhorrent to anyone professing Christ as his or her Savior. Many people claiming to be believers, however, place their politics above their faith and help enact ungodly laws that injure the Christian faith. In reality, these *so-called* followers of Christ are spitting in the face of God. They essentially are saying God and godliness be damned; my politics take priority.

10

THE RAPTURE OF THE CHURCH?

PEOPLE ARE DIVIDED ON THIS ISSUE, BUT MOST THEOLOGIANS teach that the Second Coming of Jesus will unfold in two separate events—first, the rapture of the Christian Church and then the ***Second Coming of Jesus*** as He physically returns to the earth. Most churches teach that seven years prior to the actual Second Coming of Jesus, the Lord will appear in the air, not on the earth, and He will rapture the saints of God. Rapture theology initially was rejected by virtually all theologians, but it became popular and gained wide acceptance in the 1800s after frequent teachings of this doctrine by John Darby of the Plymouth Brethren.

There aren't any verses of Scripture that explicitly expound the theory of the rapture of the Christian Church. I must admit that I lean heavily toward the Second Coming of Christ to the earth happening in one event, without believers being raptured first. I believe the rapture is possible, but it is not absolutely guaranteed by Scripture. No one knows definitively that the ***Second Advent of Christ*** will occur in two events—the rapture of saints and then the physical appearance of Jesus upon the earth.

There have been a series of LEFT BEHIND books written on the subject of the rapture and what might ensue after followers of Christ are removed from the earth. Many Christians are absolutely absorbed by the idea of the rapture. If the rapture happened today, however, I believe people would be greatly surprised at the number of apostate churches and nonbelievers attending Christian churches who would be left behind. While we should look forward to the return of Christ, the Lord tells us in Luke 19:13 to "occupy until He comes." In other words, Jesus says that we are to concentrate on investing in God's Kingdom until He returns. We also are told to look forward to His return, but not to fixate on the Second Advent of Christ.

Concentrating too much on being raptured in order to escape the chaos happening on the earth could cause some of us to miss out on what God has purposed for us to do here. Our motivation should be to become mature in Christ and make disciples of other people. The early disciples of Jesus, often at great risk, promoted the Gospel and invested heavily in helping others—while still hoping for the return of Christ.

I'm unable to find any evidence in the Scriptures that the early Church believed in a rapture of the saints prior to the Second Advent of Christ. It is true that many of the disciples clearly believed that Jesus would return during their lifetimes—in the first century. It's curious, however, when the disciples asked Jesus in Matthew 24:3

what would be the sign of His coming and the end of the age, that Jesus never mentioned a rapture taking place prior to Him physically returning to the earth.

The rapture seems like a pretty monumental event! Yet, Jesus doesn't mention it at all. Jesus relates to His disciples many things that will take place before He returns, such as wars and rumors of war, nations and kingdoms rising up against each other, famines and earthquakes occurring in various places, disciples being killed for their faith, false prophets and false christs performing signs and wonders, prevalent lawlessness, great tribulation, etc. But Jesus never reassures His disciples that they will be spared any of these things, nor does He console us by telling believers to look for a rapture of the Christian Church in order to escape these future perilous events that will happen on the earth at the end of the age. Jesus does indicate, however, in Matthew 24:29–30, that immediately after the dark days of tribulation that He has just described to His disciples, He will appear in heaven, and people will see Him coming on the clouds of heaven with power and great glory. In Matthew 24:31, He further states that He will send His angels to gather His elect from the four winds, from one end of heaven to the other. But the "gathering of the saints" is described as happening after the great tribulation takes place upon the earth—not before these horrible events happen. Again, when the disciples question Jesus about the sign of His coming and the end of the age, Jesus never describes a rapture of the Christian Church prior to His physical return to the earth.

Theologians quote several Scriptures in order to prove their hypotheses of the rapture of the saints. The most quoted Scriptures are 1 Thessalonians 4:15–17 and Revelation 3:10. First

Thessalonians, chapter 4, refers to Jesus appearing in the clouds. Revelation 3:10 indicates that the Lord will spare Christians from the hour of trial. Most, if not all, of the other Scriptures often referenced by theologians clearly reveal the Second Coming of Jesus Christ, but not necessarily a rapture of the saints.

Some Scriptures frequently quoted by theologians from the book of Daniel have already been fulfilled. I believe the fulfillment of other Scriptures could happen at any time, bringing the return of Christ or *possibly* the rapture of the Christian Church. Followers of Christ believe in the Second Advent of Jesus, but not everyone agrees about the rapture. Some theologians claim wrongly that anyone not believing in the rapture will be left behind when the rapture takes place. Belief in the rapture is not a prerequisite for salvation.

Jesus definitely, unequivocally, is coming back to the earth again; this time He is coming to retrieve His bride (the Church) and to punish the wicked! Jesus is returning as the Judge, not the Redeemer. When Jesus will return cannot be known by anyone, although there have been many false prophecies declaring the date(s) of His return. Every one of these prophecies have failed and have managed to make those making these predictions appear unhinged.

The Bible indicates that there will be both tribulation and a great tribulation; however, no one knows when these events will occur (see Matthew 24:21–22; Matthew 24:29; Daniel 12:1; and Revelation 7:14). Many individuals believe Christians will be raptured and spared from both the tribulation and the great tribulation. Some theologians believe in a pre-tribulation rapture, while others believe in a mid-tribulation or a post-tribulation event. As I indicated earlier, some theologians do not believe in the rapture of believers at all.

There is a lot of confusion surrounding this issue, and there also are many misinterpreted Scriptures relating to the Second Coming. Clearly, some ministers of the Gospel are right about this issue. Others are confused and are teaching a false doctrine. Who's right and who's wrong? That is the question. We all agree that Jesus is coming back to judge sinners and retrieve His people, but whether this happens in one or two events is debated among Christians.

The Bible says that no one knows the day or hour when Christ is returning, but that we may know the season by the things happening upon the earth (see Matthew 24:36 and Mark 13:32). At the same time, the Scriptures indicate that the return of Christ will be like a thief appearing in the night (see 1 Thessalonians 5:2; 2 Peter 3:10; and Revelation 16:15). Many people will be caught off guard, won't understand the signs of the times, and will have no idea what is about to take place.

11

REVIVED ROMAN EMPIRE AND THE POPE IS THE ANTICHRIST?

SOME THEOLOGIANS TEACH, AS ABSOLUTE FACT, THAT THERE will be a revived Roman Empire before the Second Advent of Jesus Christ. They also teach that the pope is the false prophet or the Antichrist. However, not everyone agrees with this doctrine. There's no evidence in the Scriptures that the ancient Roman Empire will be revived before the return of Christ, nor is there any indication that the last serving pope at the return of Christ will be either the false prophet or the Antichrist mentioned in the book of Revelation. This doctrine has been taught for centuries, but it was *never* taught in the early Church.

Some historians and theologians claim that the ancient Roman Empire is still in existence today; however, it can be proven historically that the western portion of the Roman Empire fell many centuries ago. The eastern portion of the Roman Empire continued for many years after the fall of the western portion, but it, too, eventually fell.

Again, there's no clear Scripture to validate the belief that the Roman Empire will be revived. I'm not saying that it's an impossibility, nor am I saying that the pope and the Roman Catholic Church won't play a role in end-time prophecy. But I have studied the Scriptures and end-time prophecy extensively, and I find no evidence to support either of these claims. However, prophecy in the book of Revelation and other unfulfilled Scriptures is about as clear as mud to most people.

I heard one of my favorite theologians once say that he rarely preached on the book of Revelation, because he didn't understand it. He also indicated that nobody else understands it either, and those who claim to understand end-time events are being dishonest. So much of end-time doctrine can neither be proven definitively or disproven with absolute certainty. All we know for sure is that Jesus is returning and that He and His saints win in the end! The most important thing we can do is to be ready when Christ returns.

Rather than concentrating on speculation of what the book of Revelation means, we should ensure that we have a sincere relationship with the Lord—then we won't we caught in the same trap as the five foolish virgins described in the parable found in Matthew 25:1–13. We would be wise to live as the apostle Paul did, who stated that he always strived to have a conscience without offense toward God and men (see Acts 24:16).

So much confusion surrounds the issue of the false prophet and the Antichrist. There has been much conjecture over the years as to who these individuals might be and how best to identify them. I can remember some theologians speculating that President John F. Kennedy was the Antichrist. When he was assassinated, some delusional ministers thought JFK would be resurrected from the dead, especially because he died from a mortal wound to his head. I also heard people claiming that President Ronald Wilson Reagan might be the Antichrist, because he had three names containing six letters each—thus equating to the number 666 (see Revelation 13:18).

These claims were outrageous! Nobody knows who the false prophet or Antichrist are, but they'll be clearly known when they eventually show up. Then no one will be guessing as to their identities. Until that time, foolish speculation only makes Christians appear unhinged and helps to discredit the Christian Church. Our goal, as believers, should be to attract nonbelievers, not drive them away from the Gospel of Christ by appearing deranged. The enemy is using questionable theories to distract believers from their main focus of serving Christ and making disciples of men.

12

CHRISTIANS ARE ALWAYS HEALED?

IT'S TRUE THAT HEALING WAS PROVIDED FOR IN THE SACRIFICE of Jesus Christ on the cross (Isaiah 53:5). However, the teaching that Christians are **always** healed is not a valid doctrine. I cannot imagine anyone accepting this belief without realizing that there are no two-thousand-year-old people still living today. Surely, most reasonable individuals can see the fallacy of this teaching. One need only ask: How many people are permanently healed and still roaming the earth today?

Theologians who teach the *always healed* doctrine will grow old and die someday themselves. Even those who are healed today will eventually die. Currently, the mortality rate is 100 percent. Absolutely nobody lives forever. The many people whom Jesus healed and those healed during the ministry of the early apostles ultimately also died.

I believe in divine healing, and I've been a very joyful recipient of healing more than once in my life. However, this does not mean that **all** Christians are **always** healed. We should pray in faith for healing, but we also must realize that not all individuals will be healed. Unless Christ returns while we're still living physically on the earth, all of us are going to die someday. The Bible indicates that people are destined to die once and then face the judgment (see Hebrews 9:27). This applies to virtually all individuals; they generally *die once.*

A few people actually have died and been restored to life, but in the end they die again. Not a single person lives forever. We all have a destiny with death, unless the Lord returns before we die. Nobody is getting out of this life alive—unless they're living when Jesus returns. Even then, their bodies will be changed and glorified, because flesh and blood cannot inherit the Kingdom of heaven (1 Corinthians 15:50). Believers will be healed and perfected permanently in heaven.

Only two individuals in ancient biblical history ever made it to heaven without dying—Enoch and Elijah. But the Bible seems to indicate that they will return to the earth at the end of the age and will then be killed physically. Not even Jesus made it back to heaven without dying physically.

Again, I believe in divine healing. It clearly is provided for in the atonement of Jesus Christ, so we should pray for those who are ill or hurting. The Lord does not desire that His children be in pain and suffering. But we also must hear from the Lord concerning whether to pray for a person's healing. God may be calling an individual home to be with Him. At other times, a prayer for healing may be useless, if a person holds unforgiveness in his or her heart or if the person doesn't have the faith for their healing.

Praying for healing also is futile if an individual is living a lifestyle that isn't conducive to healing. I once saw a famous female evangelist being filmed grocery shopping; she had been diagnosed with cancer, and she was making the effort to change her eating habits. She first filled her shopping cart with healthy foods that might help her survive cancer. Then she put all the healthy alternatives back and filled her shopping cart with unhealthy foods sure to cause her even more health issues. Not surprisingly, she died from cancer a short time later.

Physicians frequently advise people to modify their diets and change their unhealthy behavior in order to prevent illness or premature death, but often individuals don't listen to their doctor's advice. It would be useless to pray for healing for people rejecting sound medical advice. The fervent prayer of a righteous person avails much (James 5:16), but it's not a cure for irrational behavior.

13

ALL CHRISTIANS SHOULD BE WEALTHY?

ANOTHER ERRONEOUS TEACHING IN MANY CHURCHES IS THAT *all* Christians are to be enormously wealthy. This is known as the ***prosperity gospel.*** Some ministers, especially those who often fleece the flock, teach that all Christians should be extremely wealthy.

Some of the worst violators teach that if people send them a big ***seed offering,*** God will bless them with a huge return on their investment. The promise from these dishonest ministers guarantees a big return on an offering, much better than a high-yield stock. Not all theologians preaching prosperity are dishonest people; some of them sincerely believe what they're teaching and acquire enormous wealth.

It is true that the Bible does teach Christians to pay tithes and give offerings to their local churches and to charities (see Malachi

3:10). Also, read Luke 21:1–4, where Jesus commends a poor widow for giving two mites in the offering. The rich gave from their abundance—not impressive—but the poor widow gave even though she was poverty-stricken.

Malachi 3:8–9 informs us that we're robbing God, if we don't tithe. We're instructed to tithe and give offerings; however, there is no guarantee that a person who allows themselves to be fleeced by unscrupulous preachers will automatically gain a huge financial return. The Lord expects us to use wisdom in the type of church we attend and also in the types of charities and ministries we support financially. There have been a few charities and ministries that we decided not to support after learning that they weren't good stewards of the financial contributions we gave to them.

I definitely believe the Lord desires that all His children live comfortably. However, this doesn't necessarily equate to all Christians being enormously prosperous. Some individuals make unwise decisions concerning their finances. Others are disobedient to the Lord, hoarding their resources or never tithing or helping the poor and less fortunate. These individuals are a bit like the rich young ruler described in Matthew 19:16–22, Mark 10:17–22, and Luke 18:18–23. Still other Christians have wrong motives for paying tithes and giving offerings. They may give selfishly specifically in order to gain wealth.

Demonic powers also motivate some Christians to give to the wrong kind of causes, such as Black Lives Matter or other liberal foundations. The Lord expects us to be good stewards of the resources He has entrusted to us. See the parables in Matthew 25:14–30 and Luke 19:11–27 describing how we are to manage our financial assets. Those who fail to steward their resources properly are called evil servants by the Lord.

Both the gospels of Matthew and Luke warn Christians that they will be judged by the way in which they manage what the Lord has given them. Unlike those who want to redistribute wealth to lazy individuals who won't work, Jesus says to give more to those who have worked hard and have managed their finances wisely. In the economy of Jesus, wise stewards should receive more since they can be trusted with finances.

Christians are to give and help provide for impoverished people, but they're not instructed to give to those who are lazy and won't work. In fact, the Bible essentially says not to feed individuals who are too lazy to provide for themselves (see 2 Thessalonians 3:10–12). Some individuals live in abject poverty due to no fault of their own. These are the people whom we are to assist.

We are advised in various Scriptures to help those less fortunate and not to be greedy or hoard what we have acquired. Matthew 19:23–24, Mark 10:23–25, and Luke 18:24–25 warn how difficult it is for rich people to enter the Kingdom of heaven. Further, Luke 12:21 states: "Yes, a person is a fool to store up earthly wealth but not have a rich relationship with God" (NLT). In other words, Christians are not to chase after money and strive for wealth, but rather they are to develop an intimate relationship with the Lord.

A right relationship with the Lord is far better than earthly wealth, which is temporal and will fade away. We are to be rich toward God and help others. It's truly grievous to see so many impoverished and hurting people throughout the world today, and so many ungodly people with great wealth who won't help them.

The vast majority of these hurting people are helped by kind, sacrificing Christians. I'm grieved to see the abject poverty of so many Native Americans who have been forgotten by our government and other citizens of the United States.

There were many impoverished Christians in the early Church. Some of the wealthy Christians sold their property to provide for the financial needs of others. Also, frequently offerings were collected to assist the poor (see Acts 4:34–35; Romans 15:26–27; 1 Corinthians 16:1–3; 2 Corinthians 8:3–4; and Galatians 2:10). Jesus never taught His disciples to seek wealth, but rather to seek God (see Matthew 6:33).

There are many other Scriptures that encourage us to manage our financial resources wisely. For example, Matthew 6:19–21 instructs us: "Do not lay up for yourselves treasures on earth, where moth and rust destroy and where thieves break in and steal; but lay up for yourselves treasures in heaven, where neither moth nor rust destroys and where thieves do not break in and steal. For where your treasure is, there your heart will be also."

We are not to be like the man whose crops yielded so much that he didn't have enough storage space in his barns, so he decided to pull down his barns and build larger ones (see the parable in Luke 12:16–20). We also aren't to follow the example of the rich young ruler who kept all the commandments, but was so attached to his wealth that he failed to follow Jesus.

Most Christians aren't filthy rich like the rich young ruler described in the Bible, or like dishonest U.S. politicians or Russian oligarchs who own multiple mansions, luxury yachts, and private jets. As I indicated earlier, some individuals attain wealth and hoard it, never helping those who are less fortunate. Some unsavory people attain wealth dishonestly, many times taking advantage of others and never helping the poor or disadvantaged.

If we give, we are promised to receive in the same measure in which we give (see Luke 6:38). This can apply to monetary wealth, as well as to other things, such as the kindness and mercy shown to others. We also can reap unpleasant things, if that is what we've sown. We will reap that which we have sown—whether good or bad things. It appears that many wicked people get away with doing wrong and never reap what they sow, but they will reap eventually in this life or in the life to come.

Actually, I find it disconcerting to see many individuals seemingly getting away with evil and living in opulence when so many people in the world are starving. It's not just disconcerting, but obscene! I realize, however, that God will deal with these selfish individuals someday and will reward them according to their vile deeds.

As I've already noted, many Scriptures indicate that we are to give financial resources to help people in need. But again, there's no guarantee of fame and fortune for doing so. We also are instructed to love, show mercy, and forgive others. The same measure in which we do these things is the same measure that we will receive—either in this life or at the final judgment of Christ.

14

MORE THAN ONE ROAD LEADS TO HEAVEN?

I AM ABSOLUTELY SHOCKED THAT ANYONE CLAIMS MULTIPLE roads lead to God and heaven. This teaching is diabolically false! People promoting the *multiple roads* theory are grossly dishonest and are leading gullible people totally astray. The Bible is clear that **Jesus** is the **only way** to God and heaven.

Jesus states in John 10:9: "I am the door. If anyone enters by Me, he will be saved." In the gospel of John, Thomas questioned Jesus about where He was going and the way in which He was going. Jesus responded to Thomas in John 14:6, stating that He (Jesus) is the way, the truth, and the life, and that no one comes to the Father except through Him. Further, John 3:36 says: "He who believes in the Son has everlasting life; and he who does not believe the Son shall not see life, but the wrath of God abides on him." Jesus further states in John 6:47: "Most assuredly, I say to you, he who believes in Me has everlasting life." These Scriptures make it crystal clear that people cannot gain eternal life without accepting Jesus as their Savior.

Matthew 7:13–14 states: "Enter by the narrow gate; for wide is the gate and broad is the way that leads to destruction, and there are many who go in by it. Because narrow is the gate and difficult is the way which leads to life, and there are few who find it." The narrow gate is Jesus. These and many other Scriptures make it clear that ***Jesus is the only way*** to heaven and to eternal life.

There is no other way to attain eternal life; the Lord Jesus Christ is absolutely, positively the only way! Many roads do not lead to heaven. Several Scriptures inform us that we cannot have the Father without accepting Jesus. Some false religions relegate Jesus to being a real nice guy, a minor prophet, or a pretty good dude. But Jesus cannot be reduced to just a good person; He is the only road leading to eternal life.

Many false religions don't recognize Jesus at all. For example, Hinduism has thirty-three million gods. This religion has both minor gods and major gods. Imagine millions upon millions of gods—how utterly confusing!

I asked a young lady from India once why she had a small wooden figure sitting on the dash of her car. She explained that her father had given her this god to help protect her and keep her safe while she was employed in the United States. She told me that she didn't really believe in the tiny wooden god, but she kept it in order to honor her father. I thought how incredibly sad it was that anybody on earth could still believe that a wooden idol (god) could help protect anyone.

By the way, parents should be very careful concerning what children's films they allow their young kids to watch. Liberals in the entertainment industry often sneak false gods and other inappropriate materials into children's movies nowadays. So be forewarned that there are many false teachers and false prophets in the film industry, as well as in apostate churches today!

Again, there are *not* many ways to God. There is one way only, and that way is Jesus Christ—period! A person cannot get to God through religion, by their good deeds, or by their own intellect. Some people say they are Christians because they believe in God—big deal. The devil and demons believe in God and tremble (see James 2:19).

The only way to God is to get out of Adam (fallen man) and get into Christ the risen Savior. Every person on earth right now is either in Adam or in Christ. If Jesus Christ doesn't live in a person, then they are still dead in their sins, and the wrath of God abides on them (John 3:36). Essentially there are only two races of people on earth, the one that is in Christ and the race that is still in Adam. This is one reason that it's so foolish to divide over race. The color of a person's skin is unimportant in God's Kingdom. The only important and qualifying factor is whether an individual has moved out of the race of Adam and into Christ.

Even illiterate people or people who have never heard the Gospel sometimes have come to know the Lord, moving from Adam into Christ. People are without excuse for not knowing the Lord Jesus Christ. In His mercy, God has given some people visions and dreams of Jesus—leading them to Christ. Also, through creation God has made Himself known to all men. People can know the

Lord, if they truly desire to know Him. Some of them just need a little push sometimes, like churches and crusades holding altar calls and asking folks to repent of their sins. The Lord calls to every single individual, because His sincere desire is that no one perish. Often people don't hear Him call, because there's too much noise bombarding them from other people and other places.

Many people accept the historical Jesus but not the life of Christ. A mere mental assent of Christ isn't knowing Him. Individuals must repent of their sins and accept the sacrifice of Jesus to be born-again believers. God will reveal Christ to people, and Jesus will reveal the Father to anyone who seriously wants to know the truth. People can ask for a revelation of truth. Knowing about Jesus isn't the same as knowing Him intimately. Also, just learning historical facts about the Lord is not a road that leads to eternal life.

Many roads do not lead to God; however, there are multiple ways in which to discover Him—responding to an altar call after hearing the Gospel, gaining knowledge of God through reading the Bible and accepting Christ on one's own initiative, or becoming a believer after having a dream or vision of Jesus. The *multiple roads* gospel is a false doctrine that can only be defeated by becoming a true believer in Christ Jesus.

15

UNIVERSALISM—EVERYONE IS SAVED?

An extremely dangerous false doctrine that has crept into some churches by very deceitful teachers is that of universalism. What exactly is the doctrine of universalism? In a nutshell, this theology teaches that in the end, everybody will be saved. No need to worry. Individuals who live lives of gross sin and never accept Jesus as their Savior will still be saved. This is a diabolical corruption of the Scriptures.

Universalism isn't even remotely biblical, and in reality it does away with much of the Scripture. Universalists teach that there is no wrath of God. According to them, God won't condemn anyone to hell, and the mercy of God is endless—even extending to the vilest sinners. No hell and no punishment whatsoever for godless sinners definitely isn't what the Bible says. Other misguided theologians teach that universalism applies to Jews only; everybody else is required to become a born-again believer to be saved. This teaching is a horrific misinterpretation of Romans 11:25–26.

Jesus frequently taught about judgment, hell, and punishment for sinners, plus He spoke often of grace, salvation, and heaven being extended to believers. Jesus told a religious ruler named Nicodemus in the gospel of John that a person has to be born again in order to see the Kingdom of God (see John 3:3). The Lord also made it clear in Mark 16:16, John 3:18, John 3:36, John 5:24, John 6:47, Acts 2:38, Romans 10:9, and in a number of other Scriptures what individuals must do to inherit eternal life. By the way, Nicodemus was a Jew.

The Lord provides a stern warning to sinners about hell in Matthew 10:28. Further, Romans 6:23 says: "For the wages of sin is death, but the free gift of God is eternal life in Christ Jesus our Lord" (NASB). This Scripture is referring to spiritual death taking place in the life of individuals who don't repent of their sins. Eternal life is reserved *only* for genuine believers.

Several Scriptures list a number of sins that offend God. For example, 1 Corinthians 5:11, Ephesians 5:3–5, and 2 Timothy3:2–5 all specify sins that are offensive to the Lord. First Corinthians 6:9–10 enumerates specific sins that offend God and will keep individuals out of heaven: "Or do you not know that the unrighteous will not inherit the kingdom of God? Do not be deceived; neither fornicators, nor idolaters, nor adulterers, nor effeminate, nor homosexuals, nor thieves, nor the covetous, nor drunkards, nor revilers, nor swindlers, will inherit the kingdom of God" (NASB).

Clearly, ungodly people will not be saved. They will stand before the Lord and answer for their godless behavior. It's clear from

1 John 3:7–8 that anyone who practices righteousness is a righteous person, but those practicing unrighteousness are of the devil. The Scriptures warn people over and over again that the atoning work of Christ is received only when individuals repent and accept Jesus as their Savior. This is the only way to salvation and to be welcomed into God's Kingdom.

Individuals who won't teach the truth are insincere and are doing grave damage to the souls of gullible people. People promoting the concept of universalism are false prophets who are trusting in doctrines of demons. We are warned frequently not to allow anyone to deceive us. First John 4:1 states: "Beloved, do not believe every spirit, but test the spirits, whether they are of God; because many false prophets have gone out into the world." People must test what they're being taught to ensure it lines up with the Word of God, and to ensure they're not following false teachers.

16

THE GIFTS OF THE SPIRIT HAVE CEASED?

Many theologians teach that the gifts of the Spirit passed away with the last apostles of Jesus, while some ministers teach that only certain gifts of the Spirit are invalid today. I believe these concepts were authored by the devil in order to separate believers along denominational lines and weaken the power of the Church. It was never the desire of the Lord to have His children separated in this manner. Christians are to be united as one body under one head—the Lord Jesus Christ.

There's no indication in the Scriptures that there has been a cessation of the gifts, nor is there anything to suggest that believers should be divided into various denominations. Christians should be united as one Church and one people.

The gifts of the Spirit generally are recognized as the nine gifts identified in 1 Corinthians 12:7–10: the word of wisdom; the word of knowledge; faith; gifts of healing; working of miracles; prophecy; discerning of spirits; different kinds of tongues; and interpretation of tongues. These gifts are distributed to individuals as the Lord wills. Some theologians teach that other abilities such as administrations and helps also are gifts of the Spirit.

First Corinthians 12:28 states: "And God has appointed in the church, first apostles, second prophets, third teachers, then miracles, then gifts of healing, helps, administrations, and *various* kinds of tongues" (NASB). First Corinthians, chapter 12, provides a fairly detailed explanation of the gifts and abilities of the Spirit.

First Corinthians, chapter 13, is known as the love chapter, and it denotes the importance of following love. First Corinthians, chapter 14, further instructs Christians to pursue love but at the same time to desire spiritual gifts. As I stated previously, there is no indication that any of the gifts of the Spirit have ceased. The concept that there has been a cessation of some gifts, such as speaking in tongues, healing, miracles, and prophecy has no scriptural basis whatsoever.

Unfortunately, some people have caused confusion by misusing the spiritual gifts. This has led many individuals to question or even fear the gifts of the Spirit. Some people flee in the opposite direction at the mere mention of some of the gifts of the Spirit. For instance, speaking in tongues frightens some believers. Also, self-proclaimed prophets who prophesy events that never happen have caused many people to question their faith and others to reject Christianity altogether. I find these prophets very irritating. I can always tell that they're lying, but many gullible Christians cling to their every word! Unfortunately, the lying prophets cause true prophets to be discredited. As believers, we must test the spirits to ascertain the real from the fake. But we shouldn't discount genuine spiritual experiences, because of the bad behavior of some individuals. Real or fake experiences are spiritually discerned.

First Corinthians 2:14 says: "But the natural man does not receive the things of the Spirit of God, for they are foolishness to him; nor can he know them, because they are spiritually discerned." Further, 1 Corinthians 3:16 states that we are the temple of God and that the Spirit of God dwells in us. Many Christians live in the natural rather than the spiritual realm, and they are unaware of the gifts. These individuals won't possess the gifts of the Spirit when they're not even aware that they exist. Also, some Christians aren't aware that the Spirit of God resides within them.

Due to some excesses and extreme emotionalism, some believers are actually afraid of being baptized in the Holy Spirit and operating in the gifts of the Spirit. I am very grateful that I speak in tongues and can pray the perfect will of God in situations when I don't know what to pray. I'm also thankful that the Lord has blessed me with the gifts of discerning of spirits and the word of knowledge, which has helped protect me from spiritual error.

17

SICKNESS IS A PUNISHMENT FROM GOD?

SOME PEOPLE TEACH THAT ALL SICKNESS IS PUNISHMENT FROM God for sins. If this doctrine were even remotely true, then it would apply to everyone equally. So, how can anyone believe that a tiny baby is ill because it has somehow offended God and is being punished due to its sin? Surely, people can see the fallacy of this doctrine.

When Jesus was asked in the gospel of John who had sinned—the blind man or his parents—Jesus said that neither of them had sinned (see John 9:1–3). So it's clear that the Bible teaches that illness is not necessarily caused by a person's sin. There are, of course, times when sin does open the door for the devil to afflict us. Sin can give the devil the legal right to attack us with illness and other problematic issues.

In the Old Testament, the Lord frequently did indicate that His people (adults) were plagued with illnesses due to their disobedience. When they humbled themselves, repented, and prayed, they often were healed. In the New Testament, believers are advised in James 5:14 to ask the elders of the Church to pray over them when they're ill. Further, James states in verse 15 that the prayer of faith will heal the sick, and if the individuals have committed sins, they will be forgiven. It appears that some people do become ill because of sin, but certainly this isn't the case for all individuals.

The Lord doesn't give us cancer, liver disease, or other illnesses to punish us for sins. Sometimes we bring these things upon ourselves. Poor health habits cause many of our illnesses, and sometimes genetics also plays a role in our health. For example, certain diseases such as breast cancer and high blood pressure are hereditary in nature. However, hereditary illnesses often can be overcome by following a proper diet and by praying over genetic issues.

Several years ago, I opened my big mouth and spoke a curse upon my health. I became very ill, and nothing seemed to help. Even after seeing a physician and taking all the prescribed medication, I was still very ill. In fact, my health continued to grow worse to the point that I felt as if I would die.

A short time before I became ill, my husband was sick with the flu. He coughed and hacked without covering his mouth, even though I repeatedly reminded him not to spread the germs to me. When he didn't respond to my requests, I became angry and said,

"Well, I guess I'll just get sick and die like your mother did!" Several years before this incident, my husband's mother had become very ill with the flu and never recovered.

After a few days, I had forgotten all about this outburst. When I became ill and was unable to recover, I finally asked the Lord to reveal the problem to me. The Lord promptly reminded me of my angry outburst. The Holy Spirit spoke to me and told me that I had become ensnared by my own lips, and He reminded me of the exact words that I had spoken previously. Once I remembered the words that I had said, I repented and immediately began to recover from the illness.

The Bible tells us that we can be ensnared by the words that we speak. The first part of Proverbs 18:21 states: "Death and life are in the power of the tongue" (KJV). Also, Proverbs 17:22 says: "A merry heart does good, like medicine, but a broken spirit dries the bones." Many people who are sick have unknowingly spoken illnesses upon themselves.

I'm also convinced that many individuals suffering from arthritis and other aches and pains have broken spirits and sad hearts. Some people's spirits were crushed by words that were spoken to them by parents, teachers, or other adults while they were still young children. Many people are ill and disheartened from listening to negative words being spoken by dishonest journalists, liberals on social media, radical government leaders, and other untrustworthy individuals.

The Bible is replete with advice concerning the power of our spoken words and the importance of words spoken to us by others. Remember: Jesus spoke galaxies into existence, and all things are still held together by the power of His words. Our words are powerful, too. The words of other people also are powerful enough to create either joy or pain. Whoever coined the old adage *"Sticks and stones will break my bones, but words will never hurt me"* didn't know what he was talking about!

Many individuals in our country and other countries around the world have broken spirits and unhappy hearts today. I know it may be difficult for people living in the United States, Canada, Australia, and other countries or continents that have been taken over by radicals to remain cheerful and positive nowadays. Many people have lost hope in the midst of woke radicalism, causing them to become physically ill or turn to drugs and alcohol to try to cope, but turning to harmful substances isn't the answer. Remember: Jesus is the answer, and God didn't create the mess that we're now experiencing. Most of the things we suffer through are manmade. But if we call upon the Lord, He will answer us. Jesus promises to give us peace in the midst of life's chaos.

18

NO MORE GENERATIONAL CURSES?

Some theologians claim that generational curses no longer exist and were done away with during Old Testament times, while others teach that these types of curses still exist today. Those who teach that generational curses no longer exist quote Jeremiah 31:29 and Ezekiel 18:2 as the basis for their theology. Jeremiah and Ezekiel essentially state that the children's teeth will no longer be set on edge due to their fathers eating sour grapes—their fathers' sins. The verses following these two Scriptures say that children will not die for the sins of the fathers and vice versa. In other words, people will be judged and die for their own sins. However, other Scriptures seem to indicate that children will be plagued by the iniquities of their parents.

This is certainly true in the natural realm, and it seems to apply in the spiritual realm as well. We often see immoral parents produce immoral children. Addictive and ungodly behaviors seem to be passed on to subsequent generations. Psychologists would likely explain this as learned behaviors or conditioned responses by children who are brought up in these types of environments.

Whether curses are passed on to subsequent generations is questioned by many theologians. Nonetheless, problematic issues seem to perpetuate themselves in many families, from generation to generation. No one can deny that problems such as drug addiction, alcoholism, sexual immorality, poverty, child neglect, spousal abuse, divorce, and other serious issues seem to afflict families generationally.

As I stated previously, some theologians teach that generational curses still operate in families today. But they believe these curses can be broken in the lives of believers by prayer and righteous living.

There are many Scriptures in the Old Testament that indicate the Lord holds the iniquities of the fathers against their ungodly children. At the same time, there are other Scriptures indicating that a parent's iniquities can be overcome by the godliness of the children. In other words, if their children become believers, then they are released from the sins of their fathers (see Exodus 20:5–6; Exodus 34:6–7; Leviticus 26:39–42; Numbers 14:18; Deuteronomy 7:9; and Deuteronomy 5:9–10).

Numbers 14:18 states: "The LORD is longsuffering, and of great mercy, forgiving iniquity and transgression, and by no means clearing the guilty, visiting the iniquity of the fathers upon the children unto the third and fourth generation" (KJV). Leviticus 26 indicates that individuals will be punished for their father's iniquities, but they will be spared if they confess those sins and repent. Although iniquities are remembered unto the third and fourth generations, the Bible says that God's mercy is extended to the righteous for a thousand generations.

Deuteronomy 7:9 states: "Therefore know that the LORD your God, He is God, the faithful God who keeps covenant and mercy for a thousand generations with those who love Him and keep His commandments." The Lord declares in Deuteronomy 5:9–10 that He visits the iniquities of fathers upon the children of those who hate Him, but He shows mercy to those who love Him.

If generational curses do indeed exist, they can be broken when a person is born again. I personally believe generational curses exist, and that theologians who deny them are teaching false doctrine. However, curses can be defeated easily by applying the blood of Jesus to undesirable circumstances in a believer's life. It appears some Christians are afflicted by generational curses, because the wicked one knows they're unaware that they're being plagued by generational curses that can be broken by prayer.

Once people become born-again believers, the enemy has no legal right to impose curses upon them for iniquities committed by their parents—unless they open a door for the devil to afflict them. We must remember that just because the devil has no legal right doesn't mean that he won't attempt to harm or deceive us. The devil is always relentlessly on the job—to kill, to steal, and to destroy (John 10:10). Remember: What people don't know can harm them.

Unless Christians recognize their right to take authority over the devil, he may impose curses upon them. I believe our family is afflicted with a generational curse relating to faithful church attendance. Our parents were always on-again, off-again churchgoers. This same trait is prevalent throughout my family unto the third generation. With prayer and righteous living, this iniquity can be broken.

Some generational issues lead to codependency problems, also known as ungodly soul ties. I won't address soul ties, except to say that I believe they exist even though many theologians claim they're nonexistent. Many people have little or no understanding of the spirit realm. I've even had Christians tell me that it's utter nonsense to believe that our words contain the power to affect life or death in our lives or the lives of other people. The Bible says our words are very powerful, and I believe it's true, for the Bible tells me so.

Our words have the power to affect us and other individuals emotionally, mentally, physically, and spiritually. That is the reason it's so important to speak and pray words contained in the Scriptures. The Bible instructs us in Philippians 4:8 to think about things that are true, noble, just, pure, good, and lovely. If we think about the proper things, then we won't speak words that are harmful and hurtful to us or others. The Bible says in Luke 6:45 that whatever is in a person's heart is what will come forth, either good or evil. Both words and actions have the ability to perpetuate issues literally for generations.

19

ALL PEOPLE ARE CREATED IN THE IMAGE OF GOD?

VIRTUALLY ALL THEOLOGIANS TEACH THAT *ALL* PEOPLE HAVE been created in the image of God. I disagree with this doctrine. The original humans (Adam and Eve) were created in the image of God, but their images became marred when they sinned in the Garden of Eden. Until Eve was deceived by the devil and until Adam listened to his wife and knowingly disobeyed God by partaking of the forbidden fruit, both Adam and Eve were created to be perfect—and they were!

By eating the forbidden fruit, they disobeyed God's clear command. This is referred to as *the fall*. After the *fall of man*, their images were marred by their disobedience and sin. Adam and Eve's disobedience caused sin to enter our world, and their sin ceded the authority they initially possessed to God's archenemy—the devil. Adam and Eve initially had two sons, named Cain and Abel. Cain killed his brother, Abel, due to jealousy; it was the first murder on earth. Then Adam and Eve had a third son named Seth.

The Bible indicates that Seth was born in the image of his father (Adam). Genesis 5:3 states: "And Adam lived one hundred and thirty years, and begot a son in his own likeness, after his image, and named him Seth." From that time until Christ returns, I believe that all people are created in the image of mankind (their parents), rather than in the image of God. The Lord gave people the ability to reproduce themselves, and He gave this same ability to plants and animals. God is still the Creator of all things, and He is still creating by His spoken word. Man cannot create anything, not a single gene or molecule. But what man can do is reproduce as God designed him to do. The Lord authorized mankind, animals, plants, and other objects to reproduce themselves based on the words spoken by God. In fact, the universe is still expanding based on the words spoken by our Lord Jesus Christ at the beginning of time. Hebrews 11:3 tells us that God created the physical things that we can see out of nothing.

The Bible clearly states that Jesus Christ is the Creator of all things, and original mankind was created in the image of God. People are still created by God, but actually being created in the image of God was lost to mankind after the *fall*. When individuals are born again, they are **re-created** in the image of God. Second Corinthians 5:17 tells us that people are created new once they believe in Christ Jesus.

I cannot accept that immoral and totally depraved people are created in the image of God. Jesus calls these people children of the devil (John 8:44). How can people be children of the devil according to Jesus, and also be created in the image of God? I don't think they can. Although Christians still have free will and the ability to sin, the Scriptures tell us that their marred Adam nature is re-created in the image of God when they become believers.

Second Corinthians 3:18 indicates that Christians are being transformed into the same image as the Lord. Ephesians 4:20–24 tells us that Christians have put off the old corrupt man, have had their minds renewed by the Spirit, and have put on the new man. Colossians 3:10 states that followers of Christ have put off the old man and have put on the new man that has been *renewed* in the image of Him who created them.

The Lord creates us in the sense that all things were originally created by God, then He commanded man, animals, and plants to reproduce themselves. Jesus spoke things into existence, and things still are being created from His spoken words. It's clear from Scripture that original mankind was created in the image of God. Then sometime after the ***fall***, mankind begun to be born in the image of their parents.

The Bible also clearly appears to indicate that ***only*** born-again believers are created (actually re-created) in God's image. Murderers, pedophiles, drug addicts, alcoholics, homosexuals, and adulterers clearly are not created in the image of God—they have been created in the image of sinful Adam.

By the way, all people are either in the first Adam (natural, sinful man), or they are in the last Adam (Jesus Christ)—re-created spiritually in the image of God. Sinners remain in the first Adam, while Christians are placed in Christ Jesus. The image of a sinful person is changed from a marred image to the image of God immediately after becoming born again.

I would like to mention here that some people refer to Jesus as the "second Adam." This is a gross misinterpretation of the Scriptures. Nowhere in Scripture is Jesus referred to as the "second Adam." In 1 Corinthians 15:45–47, Jesus is called the **last** Adam and the **second Man**. The apostle Paul continues his discourse in 1 Corinthians 15:48–49, stating that as we initially bore the image of the man of dust (Adam), we also will bear the image of the heavenly Man (Jesus).

The apostle Paul indicates in First Corinthians, chapter 15, that when people are born physically that they are born in the image of natural man, then they're formed in the image of Jesus after becoming born-again believers. We often hear people say that a child is the spitting image of their father or mother, but we never hear people remarking how children are the exact image of God.

20

WE ARE ALL GOD'S CHILDREN?

THE IDEA THAT ALL HUMAN BEINGS ARE CHILDREN OF GOD IS AN extremely erroneous theological concept. It's true that we are ALL God's *creation,* but we are NOT all God's *children.* The only children of God are those individuals who are born-again believers and sincere followers of Christ. Probably all of us have heard secular people claim that we are all God's children, and even some misguided theologians teach this false doctrine.

It is dangerous to lead people to believe that they are children of God by virtue of being born physically on the earth. When Jesus told some of the religious leaders of His day that their father was the devil, this certainly didn't sound as if Jesus believed all people were His children!

21

NEVER JUDGE ANYBODY?

THE COMMAND TO "NEVER JUDGE ANYONE" IS A FAVORITE Scripture of sinners, because by taking this command out of context—it allows them to continue in their sins. Matthew 7:1–2 states: "Judge not, that you be not judged. For with what judgment you judge, you will be judged; and with the measure you use, it will be measured back to you." These are words of Jesus. Jesus continues His teaching asking why we observe the speck in our brother's eye, while not noticing the log that is in our own eye. This teaching by Jesus is one of the most misunderstood and misquoted teachings in all the Bible.

Is Jesus really saying that we are **never** to judge anyone or anyone's actions? If so, then Jesus Himself violated His own teaching. Jesus often judged the actions of others. This teaching is referring to not judging by our own standards, and not developing a habit of judging other people hypocritically. We cannot apply our own standards to how we view other individuals and their actions. We are to judge righteously by God's standards; the key words being ***judge righteously***.

The idea of never judging anyone is ludicrous. We make judgments every day about people and their actions. We would be foolish not to do so. Imagine accepting a ride from a serial killer or serial rapist, or imagine allowing a pedophile to babysit your young children simply because you don't want to "judge" them? Also, just imagine accepting everything a dishonest politician says to avoid judging their words and actions? Clearly, Jesus never intended us to never judge anybody. That is a very dangerous and foolish concept. Yet, I've even heard renowned theologians teach this nonsense. I can state unequivocally that this is false doctrine. My advice is not to listen to anyone teaching this erroneous theory.

Sinners like to misinterpret Matthew 7:1 to help appease their consciences, but there is no valid reason for theologians to quote this Scripture out of context. Even secular police officers warn women, in particular, not to fall into the deadly trap of never judging anyone. They advise women that the way in which they judge strangers may mean the difference between staying alive or being murdered. Police officers warn women that too much compassion can get them raped and killed.

I remember several years ago right after listening to a law enforcement briefing that I saw a man leaning in a van parked at a mall. The temperature was extremely hot outside, and it would have been even hotter inside the closed van. For a brief moment, I considered approaching the van to inquire if the gentleman inside was okay. Then I remembered the law enforcement briefing, and I distinctly remember the officer's voice saying, "Misplaced compassion often gets women killed!" I made the wise decision (judgment) not to approach the van.

The teaching to never judge other people is reckless, and it should never be taught to young children. They must be told not to trust strangers and that they *should* judge the behavior of weird and criminal individuals. Some strangers and sinners try to guilt people into trusting them. We shouldn't fall for this ploy.

Although we should be cautious about being too judgmental, we shouldn't be so nonjudgmental that we never confront sinful behavior. Frequently, Jesus and His disciples found it necessary to confront sin. The Bible instructs us how to address sin gracefully, so we won't fall into the same sinful behavior as those whom we're correcting (see Galatians 6:1).

Some theologians won't confront sin nowadays, because they fear being seen as intolerant. Instead of addressing sin, these theologians quote Scriptures about judging others out of context in order to disguise their mishandling of sinful behavior. They totally ignore clear Scriptures such as 2 Timothy 4:2, which advises ministers to convince, ***rebuke,*** and exhort people by preaching and teaching them the Word of God. The Word of God itself clearly states in 2 Timothy 3:16–17 that the Scriptures are valuable for doctrine, ***for reproof, for correction,*** and for instruction in righteousness so people will know the truth, know how to behave, and be equipped for doing good works. In other words, believers should know how to behave like Christians and should adhere to sound doctrine.

We are even warned in Second Timothy to avoid those who won't teach or follow the doctrine of Christ, and to have no fellowship with people living ungodly lifestyles. But many individuals today are too timid to confront sinners with the truth; they just want to make people feel good about themselves. Allowing people to continue in their sins isn't love. We should show sinners the error of their ways and teach them how to live as children of God.

We need to judge sin harshly and expose error where and when it's being taught. In confronting sin or sinners, I don't mean that we are to be rude or unkind to individuals. We are to win sinners to Christ through love, mercy, and grace, but at the same time we should address sin and expose erroneous biblical teaching. Eternal life for individuals may depend on our honesty.

Many Christians believe that we should never expose false teachers. The apostle Paul certainly didn't teach this in the early Church. Not only did he warn against false teachers, but he also *named names*. We should expose false prophets and separate ourselves from them; we absolutely must divide over false doctrine. Anyone who vilifies clear biblical doctrine needs to be exposed in order to warn other people who might fall prey to their false teaching.

Some people teach that Jesus was so gentle and kind that He never offended anyone. This simply isn't true. People killed Jesus because He offended them. As I stated earlier, Jesus told some individuals that they were of their father, the devil. Jesus never minced words, but He told people that they were sinners who needed to repent of their sins to be saved. Jesus was both gentle and stern, depending on the circumstances, but He never compromised the truth.

Most individuals associated with organizations such as the Southern Poverty Law Center, Google, YouTube, Twitter, Meta, and many other institutions in the United States would classify Jesus and His followers as a "hate group" today. Big Tech would ban Jesus and His teachings from their platforms, claiming He was inciting violence. The CEOs and many users of these platforms would call His teachings bigoted and filled with hate speech. If Jesus were to become a scheduled speaker at Harvard, Berkeley, or some other liberal academic institution, radical students and professors would riot and not allow Him on campus.

Radicals would heckle Jesus and His followers and threaten them with bodily harm. Jesus would be physically thrown off liberal college campuses today and perhaps even beaten and stoned by sinners who would consider His speech contemptible. Radical sinners, such as these, are under the influence of the devil. This is the reason they behave and speak as the wicked one behaves and speaks. Radicals in academia, the media, politics, or whatever venue in which radicals are found speak and behave as if they're totally deranged. In making this statement, I am judging righteously.

Again, it's foolish not to judge righteously and confront sin. We should follow the examples of Jesus, John the Baptist, and other early disciples. They weren't afraid of people's opinions or of being banned from social media. John the Baptist had some fairly harsh words for some of the religious leaders of his day when they came to witness his baptism activities.

Early disciples of Jesus understood the value of judging wisely. Many Scriptures discuss the issue of judging; some indicate that we shouldn't judge others, while other Scriptures indicate that we are to judge properly. When all the Scriptures are studied in proper context, the bottom line is that we are to judge righteously, using godly standards and not our own standards when judging. Naturally, we aren't to judge others when we are committing the same misdeeds or worse sins. That is being hypocritical, and hypocrisy is strongly denounced in the Scriptures (see Matthew 7:3–5). Jesus said in John 7:24 not to judge by appearance, but to judge righteously. Well said: Don't be a hypocrite; use righteous judgment.

22

HELL MEANS ETERNAL SUFFERING FOR SINNERS?

VIRTUALLY ALL CHRISTIAN FAITHS TEACH THAT HELL IS AN eternal place of everlasting conscious torment. The Seventh Day Adventists view hell as a temporary place of suffering, not eternal suffering or everlasting torture. I believe that hell is real and that all unrepentant sinners will be sent there. But the question is: What happens to sinners in hell? I personally believe it's possible that sinners will be permanently and eternally destroyed in hell—not suffer in hellfire forever.

First, the question of whether the souls of sinners live on eternally must be settled. Some theologians believe the soul is eternal, while others believe the souls of unbelievers are resurrected and then permanently destroyed in hell. Jesus said in

Matthew 10:28: "And do not fear those who kill the body but cannot kill the soul. But rather fear Him who is able to destroy both soul and body in hell." Clearly, Jesus is able to destroy the body and soul of individuals in hell. To me, this would indicate that the souls of sinners may be completely and utterly destroyed, while the souls of saints will live on eternally. The primary question is whether or not a person's soul was created by God to be eternal.

The teaching that the soul is eternal wasn't taught in the early Church. So, the question up for debate is: Does Jesus resurrect sinners to eternal life to live in physical torment forevermore? This concept was made popular with Church fathers after Plato and Aristotle postulated the theory that the soul is eternal. The current teaching of most Christian churches is that sinners will live in eternal torment, as believers live in glory. I admit that there are several Scriptures that appear to consign sinners to eternal suffering, but there are other Scriptures that seem to indicate that sinners will be utterly, eternally destroyed.

It is difficult for many people to imagine that a loving and compassionate God resurrects sinners to live eternally in physical torment. To live eternally, one must first eat of the Tree of Life (Jesus). Adam and Eve were expelled from the Garden of Eden in order to remove the possibly of them eating from the Tree of Life and living eternally in a sinful state. Therefore, some theologians believe that this indicates that sinners will *not* be resurrected to live in a sinful, tormented, conscious state forever and ever.

I've heard Pastor Doug Batchelor (a Seventh Day Adventist) preach on the subject of hell. He teaches that flawed human beings, who aren't nearly as compassionate or loving as almighty God, wouldn't doom even a tiny mouse to eternal flames and punishment, so how can people believe that the Lord of mercy would condemn a person to burn and suffer horrifically for all eternity. As I stated previously, there are Scriptures that seem to support the concept of eternal suffering for sinners. But there are also a number of other Scriptures that appear to indicate that unrepentant sinners will be totally consumed and permanently destroyed.

Some people believe permanent destruction of sinners is the more merciful and logical conclusion relating to hell. I firmly believe that hell is real; it definitely exists; it is a horrible place; and it provides eternal punishment for sinners. Many theologians believe that the punishment of sinners possibly is eternal in the sense that sinners are doomed forever, are completely destroyed, and cannot ever be resurrected again, nor can they be converted to Christ once they die. Again, the real question appears to be whether a sinner's soul is eternal.

Clearly, once sinners die, there is no hope for them to ever be converted (born again); their fate is sealed. I know most theologians teach and believe in an eternal place of flames where sinners are consigned to consciously suffer forever. This doctrine is based primarily on the teaching of Jesus contained in Luke 16:19–31 about the rich man and Lazarus. Although the story about the rich man and Lazarus is sandwiched between numerous parables taught by Jesus, many people believe this particular story isn't a parable because it identifies a person (Lazarus) by name.

Other parables refer to people as a son, a judge, a woman, a certain man, etc. This story, if it's a parable, about hell is the only parable that actually identifies an individual in the story by name.

Although the caption above the story doesn't indicate it's a parable, I read this particular story as many other stories told by Jesus as a parable. (Captions aren't a part of the Scriptures or necessarily inspired by the Holy Spirit. Captions were added later, as were chapter numbers and the numbering of verses, to help us quickly locate information in our Bibles.)

People in the first century whom Jesus was addressing would have been familiar with the name Lazarus. Jesus was friends with Lazarus of Bethany and his family, and He had raised him from the dead. Most likely many of the people listening to Jesus would have known that Jesus had a friend named Lazarus that He had miraculously raised from the dead. After all this was big news, because Lazarus had been dead for four days when Jesus commanded him to come forth from his grave (see John 11:38–44)!

This miracle so infuriated the religious leaders that they not only sought to kill Jesus, but they wanted to kill Lazarus as well. The people to whom Jesus was speaking also probably would have heard Jesus preaching the Gospel earlier, and would have known that Jesus healed multitudes of people, cast out demons, and raised numerous people from the dead—even if some of them hadn't heard about Lazarus being raised from the dead.

Jesus sometimes presented a teaching and then told a parable to highlight the teaching, or He told a parable and then followed it with an applicable teaching. People teach that the story about the rich man and Lazarus in Luke, chapter 16, cannot possibly be a parable, because Jesus names an actual person in the story. If this is true, shouldn't the converse also be true of other stories in the Bible? What I mean by this is: Stories in the Bible about actual people (other than Lazarus) being raised from the dead aren't identified by name. Yet these are factual stories of actual events. No one claims that just because these individuals aren't identified by name, they aren't actual people or that these events didn't actually happen.

I think perhaps Jesus chose to identify the poor man (Lazarus) as being in paradise (heaven) to represent all believers, while the unnamed rich man represents sinners who'll be condemned. If the story is a parable, as I propose that it possibly is, then not every word of the parable can be taken literally. A parable is simply a story used to illustrate a point. The point being in this parable that both heaven and hell are real places, but many people even after seeing Jesus raise Lazarus and other individuals from the dead still didn't believe in Him. Even after this stern warning and the resurrection of Jesus, there were still many people in the first century who didn't trust in Him, as there are many people today who refuse to believe in Christ.

By the way, a few fringe churches teach that there is no hell, and they also teach universal salvation. These teachings are unequivocally false doctrine. There are many clear Scriptures about a literal hell where sinners will be condemned and punished. There also are many, many Scriptures indicating that there is no such thing as universal salvation. The Scriptures teach exactly the opposite of these two false concepts. I address these theories in more detail under "Universalism, Everybody Is Saved" and "Progressive Christianity."

Again, hell is a real place, where unrepentant sinners will be punished for their sins. The only way to escape this horrific place is to accept Jesus as Savior and remain faithful to Him until one physically dies. The psalmist writes in Psalm 104:35: "May sinners be consumed from the earth, and the wicked be no more." This may sound unkind and harsh, but I look forward to the Day of Judgment, when sin and sinners will be no more—no more hatred, no more violence, and no more pain. I'm looking toward that celestial city, whose builder is God.

23

SATAN IS IN CHARGE OF HELL?

MOST OF US HAVE PROBABLY HEARD THEOLOGIANS AND OTHER misguided individuals declare how the devil will torment people in hell. This is false doctrine. The devil is not in charge of hell, but rather the devil, fallen angels, the beast, the false prophet, and all sinners ultimately will be cast into the lake of fire by Jesus (see Matthew 25:41 and Revelation 20:10). For sinners, being thrown into the lake of fire is known as the "second death" (see Revelation 21:8). The devil and his angels will be tormented in hell forever and ever.

As the Creator of all things and of all mankind, only Jesus has the right to judge anyone deserving of hell. Jesus, and Jesus alone, is in charge of hell. The devil will lose all power over sinners once he is judged and cast into the lake of fire. The devil has tormented and manipulated people for centuries, but that will come to an abrupt end when he is cast into hell.

I cannot imagine any properly trained theologian seriously believing or teaching that the devil is in charge of hell. Anyone believing such an erroneous concept cannot possibly be a serious student of the Word of God. Yet, I've heard ministers describe hell as a place where the devil will torment sinners forever and ever. They sometimes even paint a very dark picture of the devil tormenting people with nasty words and torturing sinners with a sharp pitchfork-like instrument to ensure sinners roast better in the flames of hell. This portrayal of hell, the devil, and sinners sounds like a script from a B-rated movie that would be truly comical if it wasn't about such a serious subject and wasn't such a gross misrepresentation of the Scriptures. People promoting such disgusting theology appear to be unkind individuals who are using theatrics to frighten sinners.

Hell is real, and it is a terrible place that everyone should avoid by accepting Jesus as Savior. People have the ability to choose either heaven or hell. The devil doesn't have that choice; his fate was sealed long ago when he rebelled against God and was cast out of heaven.

24

DEATH ON THE CROSS IS THE CRUELEST PUNISHMENT?

SOME THEOLOGIANS TEACH THAT THE CROSS WAS THE WORST possible type of death known to man. I don't accept this belief as even remotely true. Although dying on the cross was a horrible way to die, there are far more cruel ways to die.

Individuals who speak only of the cruelty of the cross are missing the most important aspect of Jesus' death on the cross. Though the cross was cruel and unusual punishment for sure, the most horrific part of Jesus dying on the cross was that He took upon Himself all the sins of humanity.

God loved us and demonstrated His love for us by giving His Son for us, so we wouldn't perish—but have everlasting life. Imagine how horrific it must have been for the sinless Son of God to take in His body the sins of mankind—sins such as murder, rape, pedophilia, brutal beatings, adultery, worship of false gods, foul language, and the list goes on and on. When Christians understand this truth, they can only exclaim that they love Jesus!

Far too many theologians concentrate too heavily on the fact that Jesus died on the cross, and they neglect the resurrection of Christ to give new life. Two thieves died with Jesus on the cross, as did many other people during that era. Many individuals were executed on a cross and many others died in much more heinous ways in New Testament times.

Dying on the cross should not be the focal point. The message of the cross is not that Jesus died on a cross, but rather what took place on the cross and after the cross. The true message of the cross is that Jesus became sin for us on the cross—He took into His body and spirit all the sins of mankind for all time. Jesus literally became man's sin in order to take away sin, so man's fellowship with God could be restored. Second Corinthians 5:21 says: "For He made Him who knew no sin to be sin for us, that we might become the righteousness of God in Him."

God's fury at sin was satisfied, and man's fellowship with God was restored as a free gift of grace through faith. After the death of Jesus, He was raised to life again. His resurrection is what gives us eternal life by faith. Without the resurrection, people would still be in their sins and spiritually dead (see 1 Corinthians 15:17).

It is by believing in the death and resurrection of Christ that people are born again and pass over from spiritual death to eternal life (John 5:24). However, to simply believe that Jesus existed and that He rose from the dead is not enough. People often focus on the natural and miss the spiritual. People must not only believe with their intellect, but they must also believe in their hearts, repent of their sins, and accept the life of Christ in order to be born again.

Let none of us be guilty of missing the main focus of the death of Jesus on the cross and resurrection of Christ, nor the main point of salvation. Confessing, repenting, and truly believing is necessary in order to receive the grace of God to genuine salvation.

25

THE KING JAMES BIBLE IS THE ORIGINAL WORD OF GOD?

SOME THEOLOGIANS TEACH THAT THE KING JAMES VERSION (KJV) of the Bible is the original and only true version of the Word of God. They believe that any other translation of the Bible violates the verse of Scripture indicating that no one is to add to or take away anything from the Word of God (see Revelation 22:18–19). These theologians have acquired quite a following over the years. Those believing this doctrine are known as "King James Only people."

I find it a bit disconcerting, in an age where people have access to almost unlimited data, that so many individuals are so easily convinced to accept this unsound doctrine. This theory easily can be debunked simply by doing a small amount of research. Think realistically for a moment about this belief relating to the King

James Bible. While on earth, did Jesus or any of God's people in the Old or New Testaments speak or write in King James English?

The Old Testament originally was written almost exclusively in Hebrew. A few of the Scriptures in the Old Testament were written in Aramaic. The New Testament was written exclusively in the Greek language. However, ancient church fathers say that the gospel of Matthew originally was written entirely in Aramaic. The initial version of the gospel of Matthew either was lost or destroyed, and the new version was compiled in Greek. During the time of Christ and the early disciples, Greek was the *lingua franca* of that time period in history. *Koine* Greek was the common language of that day, just as English is the *lingua franca* of today.

King James of England authorized the Scriptures to be translated into English. The King James Version of the Bible was first published in 1611. Although other versions of the Bible were published either during or before that timeframe, the King James Version was the recognized authorized version by the Church of England that many theologians still use today. The King James Bible, however, was not the first Bible to be translated into English. Prior to the publication of the King James Version, there were at least four or five other Bible translations composed in the English language. For example, the Great Bible was authorized by King Henry VIII, and the Geneva Bible was published fifty-one years before the King James Version and was carried to America on the *Mayflower*. Other English translations, in whole or in part, were the Tyndale Bible, the Coverdale Bible, and the Wycliffe Bible—all of them published before the King James Bible.

To claim that the King James Bible is the original Word of God, or even that it was translated from the original manuscripts, is disingenuous. The original Scriptures do not exist today, nor did they exist when the King James Bible was being written. The original Scriptures were destroyed due to age deterioration or by war, and they had to be reconstructed. Most of the oldest known manuscripts of the New Testament date from 325 AD to 360 AD, with the exception of a fragment of the gospel of John dating back to 125 AD. Amazingly, fragments from a number of ancient manuscripts have been discovered in various centuries and in various places, including those contained in the Dead Sea Scrolls. Although the devil and evil men have tried to annihilate the Scriptures, the Lord has preserved His Word. We can still trust the Scriptures to be the inerrant Word of God.

The Dead Sea Scrolls, discovered in the 1940s, contained the complete book of Isaiah and fragments of all books of the Old Testament except for the book of Esther. The majority of these Scriptures were written in Hebrew with a few written in Aramaic. Naturally, these documents were copies of original manuscripts, some dating back to a few hundred years before Christ and a few dating to the first century BC. The Dead Sea Scrolls were a major discovery, and they help to validate the inerrancy of the Word of God. These scrolls also contained fragments of New Testament Scriptures, and other religious writings. If anyone is interested in a further study of the Dead Sea Scrolls and the history of the Bible, I recommend reading the works of Emanuel Tov, professor of Bible studies. He has completed an extensive study of the Scriptures, has authored a number of books, and has been honored by many countries with a host of awards for his outstanding works.

While the King James Bible is a good translation, it isn't based on the oldest known existing manuscripts of the Scriptures. So, it may not be the most accurate Bible on the market today. The Scriptures have been further translated into many other English versions and many other languages around the world. Not everyone in the world can read English, and not all words in the KJV can be translated word for word into foreign languages. There are some words in various languages that have no English word equivalents. This being said, it is ludicrous for people to insist that the King James Bible is the only true version of the Scriptures.

Again, Jesus nor any of His original followers spoke English, so the original Scriptures couldn't have been composed in either modern or classical English.

I encourage Christians not to become ensnared by silly beliefs that can be invalidated by a nine-year-old searching the history of the Word of God. Instead, I encourage people to think logically and critically. Some of the poetry in the King James Bible is very lovely, but much of the KJV is difficult to read. I even hear some modern-day preachers struggling and sounding almost tongue-tied when pronouncing some words in the King James language. I also think that King James Only ministers may repel potential believers who find their way into church services where the KJV is being read exclusively. Most sinners aren't going to be attracted to Scriptures they have difficulty understanding. I know this chapter will offend some King James Only people, but it contains the truth. Many KJV folks become very angrily animated when the King James translation of the Scriptures is questioned in any way. These individuals simply don't have an open mind even to investigate the truth.

I recommend reading several versions of the Bible and comparing their compositions. I personally prefer the New King James Version of the Bible, but I also read the New Living Translation, the New American Standard Bible, and the New International Version. I have read a few other versions of the Bible that I don't recommend; they are either too wordy or too simplistic for my taste. There are some translations I won't read at all, because I don't trust their accuracy. The only complaint I have with some Bible translations is that they are updated too frequently. The 1996 version of New Living Translation, in my opinion, is far superior to the updated versions. Also, the writers for some modern Bible translations have gone woke and think it's necessary to include woke ideology in the Scriptures. My recommendation is that people avoid these translations. There is no place in the Scriptures or in churches for woke theology.

But folks, the fact is that there are no original copies of any Scriptures. Fragments exist dating back to the first through fourth centuries before Christ, but most of the Scriptures date to the fourth century AD. So, any Bible translation is a copy of a copy of a copy of reconstructed Scriptures that were destroyed or damaged beyond salvation (no pun intended). The book of Isaiah found with the Dead Sea Scrolls almost perfectly mirrors the book of Isaiah that we read in our Bibles today, with only minor deviations. We can be assured that just as the Lord has preserved His people from annihilation, He also has preserved His Word.

26

THE SCRIPTURE PROHIBITS FEMALE PREACHERS?

SOME DENOMINATIONS DON'T ALLOW WOMEN TO BE ORDAINED AS ministers of the Gospel today. Theologians of these churches take certain Scriptures out of context to validate their doctrine. Probably one of the most misunderstood Scriptures relating to this subject is 1 Corinthians 14:34, which states that women are to remain silent in the churches. What many theologians don't consider, when using this particular Scripture to validate their theology, is the culture of the early Church.

In the first century, the literacy rate among women wasn't as high as that of men. This probably made it difficult for many women to understand some of the teachings of the apostle Paul.

Admittedly, some of Paul's discourse was hard to understand—even puzzling for some believers today.

Women in the first century often weren't allowed to participate in some of the same events as men, so they perhaps didn't understand proper etiquette to be used in the Church. This may have been what led to the Corinthian women asking questions and causing disturbances in the church services, so they were told to remain silent and discuss the questions that they had with their husbands at home. The "women remain silent" advice actually was provided to address disorder that was occurring in church meetings. First Corinthians 14:40 further addresses the issues by stating: "Let all things be done decently and in order."

First Timothy 2:12 states that women are to be properly adorned and that they are to remain silent and not have authority over men in churches. Again, the apostle Paul was addressing problems that were taking place within church services pastored by his young protégé, Timothy. Timothy was a youthful pastor, so Paul wrote to him concerning how to handle certain issues within his church. Evidently, women in the first century—like many women today—were dressing in a provocative manner, were overbearing and emasculating men, weren't practicing godliness, and were causing disruptions in church services. If the Scriptures being used to confront these issues absolutely unequivocally mean that women cannot teach the Word of God, then a lot of women in the early Church violated this doctrine. There were several godly women who helped spread the good news and who taught the Gospel in home churches, some of whom were highly respected by the apostle Paul.

Jesus came to liberate people, and He certainly liberated women to spread the Gospel message. There are some very excellent women ministers of the Gospel who are pastoring various churches today. Of course, as in anything else, some female pastors have become so liberated that they preach a false gospel like some of their male counterparts. To ordain or not to ordain women as preachers of the Word essentially is a church leadership personal preference issue, not a biblical issue. Other than a few Scriptures addressing cultural issues in the early Church, there don't seem to be any Scriptures prohibiting the preaching of the Gospel by females.

Most denominations that don't ordain women preachers do allow females to hold women only meetings and conferences. Often these conferences are attended by male support staff, and most of the men benefit spiritually from the excellent teachings of many of these female ministers of the Gospel.

27

GOD CONTROLS EVERYTHING ON EARTH?

THEOLOGIANS WHO TEACH THAT GOD IS IN CHARGE OF EVERYTHING happening on earth and that the will of God is always done upon the earth are either misinterpreting the Scriptures or they're reading a different Bible from the one I read. This is dangerous doctrine, because it misrepresents God and causes some individuals to distrust the Lord and blame Him for things which evil people are responsible for doing.

Misguided theologians should consider this question: Does the *doctrine of the sovereignty of God* mean that God is guilty of gross evil and responsible for murders, rapes, child molestation, sex trafficking, abortion, slavery, corrupt governments, wars, etc.? Since God cannot even be tempted by evil, He certainly cannot be responsible for these horrendous things. People do many things clearly in opposition to God's will, including rejecting Him.

The Scriptures indicate that God is sovereign, but the Bible also clearly states that God desires for all people to know Him and come to the knowledge of Christ, yet many people perish without accepting Jesus as their Savior. It appears that many individuals don't fully understand what the sovereignty of God actually means. God has given people free will to choose life with Him or to reject Him. We can't hold God responsible for what sinful mankind and demonic forces do upon the earth.

We live in a sinful, fallen world manipulated by evil men and evil forces. Surely, we cannot accuse God of things done by vile individuals being manipulated by the devil. People have the ability to choose eternal life, or they can choose sin, violence, and spiritual death.

In both Ezekiel 18:23 and Ezekiel 33:11, God expresses that He takes no pleasure in the death of the wicked. Also, both 1 Timothy 2:4 and 2 Peter 3:9 indicate that the Lord is not willing that anyone should perish, but that all would repent, come to the knowledge of truth, and be saved. God is not in charge of or responsible for our decisions or for the decisions made by sinful man.

We have free will, and we live in a grossly wicked world. If we are followers of Christ, we have the Holy Spirit to lead and guide us—but this requires our cooperation. Following the Holy Spirit usually spares us from much heartbreak and a multitude of sorrows. When believers allow the Holy Spirit to guide them, God promises to protect and shield them from the wicked one. Individuals who do not know the Lord are at the mercy of the evil one, who influences or many times controls them.

First John 5:19 tells us that unbelievers are under the sway of the wicked one. God doesn't control a person's decision to follow Him or to follow the devil—that is done by individual choice. Ungodly people frequently accuse God of every evil thing that happens on planet earth. In other words, it's God's fault that things are in such a mess. Rarely do we hear evil people accusing the devil of vile things. A lot of folks have a vague concept of the Almighty, but many of them don't even believe that there is a being called the devil. Have you noticed that the word *evil* is included in the word *devil*? The devil is the author of all evil, and he causes flawed individuals to carry out his vile plans against humanity.

I heard a theologian once say, "The will of God is rarely done upon the earth." His statement really clarified things for me. Adam and Eve originally were given authority over the earth by God, but they foolishly gave that dominion to God's archenemy. The devil has been creating chaos and wreaking all kinds of havoc upon the earth ever since that time. Dominion will be restored to its rightful owner at the end of the age, when the devil and all evil are destroyed.

Theologians who teach that God is in charge of everything evidently misunderstand the meaning of the sovereignty of God. Question: Can a sovereign, earthly king control all the thoughts and actions of all those under his reign? The answer clearly is: No. If this is true of sovereignty in the natural realm, then it's also true of sovereignty in the spiritual realm. The sovereignty of God, in a nutshell, means He is incapable of being controlled or manipulated by anyone. The Lord also is sovereign in that He is the final

Judge of all sinners and demonic forces, and nothing escapes His attention. He knows all things, but He doesn't control all things.

Since the Lord has foreknowledge of all things before they happen, He is often able to use particular circumstances for His divine purposes. Situations that appear hopeless or intended for evil, God is able to use for good. For example, Joseph was sold into slavery by his brothers, but God later used this situation to promote Joseph and save Egypt and Israel from a severe famine (see Genesis 37–50). Also, the religious rulers during the first century AD rejected Jesus and insisted that He be crucified. God used these circumstances to fulfill His purpose for Jesus to be crucified for our sins (see Acts 2:23). Many theologians point to these and other historical events in the Bible to promote the concept of the total sovereignty of God—meaning that the Lord controls everything that happens upon the earth.

The concept of sovereignty is difficult to nail down since the definition of sovereignty has changed over time. The biblical definition of sovereignty likely also has changed from its original meaning. Sovereignty perhaps can best be defined as ultimate or supreme power and authority without external control. The Lord will exercise His supreme power and authority over the new earth once sin has been abolished completely. Currently, Jesus sits at the right hand of God in heaven until all of His enemies are made a footstool for His feet (see Psalm 110:1). We are to pray for God's Kingdom to come and for His will to be done on the earth as it is in heaven (see Matthew 6:10). This prayer will not be fully realized until the end of the age when Jesus returns, all evil is destroyed, and His Kingdom is established forever.

28

NEVER RESIST THE GOVERNING AUTHORITIES?

MANY PEOPLE INSIST THAT WE MUST ALWAYS HONOR AND OBEY all political and spiritual authorities, even ungodly ones. But is this a biblical concept? Although there are Scriptures in both the Old and New Testaments that tell us to honor those in authority over us, there also clearly are times when we are to disobey those authorities. If people think about this logically, they should be able to determine, even without biblical guidance, when they should submit to political or spiritual leadership. It really is a matter of common sense, if you think about it.

Individuals should never submit to tyrannical, evil, or disillusioned leaders who vow to destroy them or their country. People must never submit to anyone who tries to force a radical worldview upon them, or anyone who tries to force them to commit evil or deny Jesus Christ. In the Scriptures, Jesus opposed religious leaders who postulated false doctrine that was injurious to the spiritual welfare of the people. Also, the apostle Peter and other early apostles disobeyed the authorities when they were forbidden to teach in the name of Jesus. In fact, Peter and the other apostles answered the religious authorities that they should obey God rather than men, and they further accused the authorities of murdering Jesus whom the apostles were preaching (see Acts 5:17–32).

In Old Testament times, it may have been less common to oppose rulers. There are, however, several instances when God's children chose to disobey ungodly commands. For example, in the book of Esther, Mordecai chose to dishonor Haman (one of the princes of Susa) by refusing to bow to him. This was a transgression of the king's command to pay homage to Haman. In the book of Daniel, three friends of Daniel refused to obey the king's order to fall down and worship the image (idol) that he had set up. Also, Daniel chose to disobey a royal statue not to pray to or petition any god or man for thirty days except for the king.

In Old Testament times, individuals who opposed political authorities could be killed, most likely beheaded, so it was particularly important to follow God's leading in dealing with tyrants during that period of history. Even a wife's life was in jeopardy, if she approached her husband (the king) without being properly summoned. Read the book of Esther.

On many occasions, God instructed His people to resist and even kill foreign kings in order to secure their safety and survival. At other times, the Lord used foreign governments to oppress and punish His people for their disobedience to Him. We must read and analyze the Word of God in context, and not try to apply any private interpretation to a single Scripture. We are to look at the whole of Scripture to understand what the Lord is saying to us about a particular issue.

If the Scriptures truly mean *never resist governmental authority* and if this theology was followed perfectly, then the United States of America wouldn't exist. I heard a Christian say once that she believed residents of the thirteen colonies violated Scripture when they resisted British rule. This individual clearly had been taught hyper-obedience to governing authority.

Many Christians today believe that we should never voice anything negative about our government leaders or oppose any laws they enact—no matter how ungodly. I am absolutely flabbergasted to hear individuals make comments about never resisting ungodly authority figures. Naturally, I know it's inappropriate to malign someone's character or try to destroy an individual's good reputation—politician or not. But we should resist and expose ungodly politicians and their godless policies. Not to do so would be dishonoring God.

People quote Romans 13:1 and 1 Peter 2:13–14 as evidence that we must always submit to governing authorities. These same Scriptures indicate that these authorities are established by God to do us good and to punish evil doers. Question: How often today do governing authorities actually reward those who live decent lives while punishing evildoers? Frequently, just the opposite takes place in our society. As the darkness continues to cover the earth and deep darkness covers the people (Isaiah 60:2), true justice is rarely being executed by our governing authorities. Often these authorities are evil men and women whose desire is to persecute godly people and suppress all conservative thought.

When dealing with the issue of either resisting or being submissive to ungodly government officials, we should consider the culture in which these particular Scriptures were written. In Old Testament times and in the early history of the Church under Roman rule, the culture was much different. God's people often were persecuted and killed for resisting human rulers, not unlike in some countries ruled by dictators today. Resistance in biblical times and in certain countries currently means individuals heads may roll—literally! In countries where brutal dictators rule, it may be wiser to pray and not confront evil rulers unless the Lord specifically asks individuals to oppose these leaders.

We are to respect positions of authority and embrace godly laws, but we don't have to agree with government officials when their worldviews and policies violate God's Word. We also do not have to agree with spiritual authorities who violate the Scriptures and ask us to disregard godliness. In fact, we must contend for the faith by voicing resistance.

It is better to obey God rather than to obey mere men. If people truly believe the concept of non-resistance as relating to government or spiritual leaders, then they will accept and embrace any ungodly thing. If they believe no resistance is biblical, then do they also believe and insist that we obey the Scriptures relating to owning slaves and slaves being obedient to their masters—ouch! I will venture to guess that the same individuals angrily insisting on a *no resistance policy* relating to authority figures would have an issue today with people owning slaves and requiring their slaves to be obedient to them.

There are a number of Scriptures in the Bible dealing with slavery. For example, Ephesians 6:5 indicates that bondservants are to be obedient to their masters, and Ephesians 6:9 exhorts masters to be kind to bondservants. Other Scriptures in the New Testament referring to bondservants or slaves being obedient to their masters and masters showing mercy to their bondservants include Colossians 3:22, Colossians 4:1, 1 Timothy 6:1–2, Titus 2:9–10, 1 Peter 2:18, and the book of Philemon. In addition to these New Testament Scriptures addressing the issue of slavery, many Scriptures in the Old Testament refer to the custom of slavery and how to treat both male and female slaves. Again, these Scriptures clearly apply to a different time in history and to a different culture when slavery was an acceptable custom.

No one in the United States would embrace slavery today—with the exception of sex slavery promoted by vile individuals. Unfortunately, our founding fathers may have interpreted the Bible to mean that slavery was an acceptable practice. Many citizens resisted their beliefs about slavery, and the horrible sin of slavery eventually was defeated. Clearly, the governing authorities during that period of our history needed to be resisted. They also needed prayer for a spiritual awakening and for a better understanding of the Scriptures.

The Bible tells us to pray for all men, for kings and all who are in authority, that we may live a quiet and peaceable life (see 1 Timothy 2:1–2). Living a peaceable life is paramount. We won't be able to live this type of life if our government leaders enact laws that impose ungodly persecution on us, our children, our grandchildren, and on the Christian Church. Anything that violates the Word of God is unacceptable and must be resisted, whether it's coming from outside or inside the Church! It is our duty to resist ungodly authorities and pray for their conversion to Christ. Then and only then can we hope to gain a quiet and peaceable life.

29

JESUS NEVER CLAIMED TO BE GOD?

INCREDIBLY, SOME PASTORS IN MAINLINE CHURCHES TODAY DO not believe in the virgin birth of Christ, and they don't believe that Jesus is the only way to the Father. They believe that individuals will be ushered into heaven based on a very loose belief in heaven and in a god of their own making. These pastors are leading their flocks totally astray by asinine doctrine that has no basis in truth at all.

Many individuals teach that Jesus was merely a good man, perhaps even a prophet—but certainly not God. Of course, a major claim of false religions is that Jesus is a pretty good dude—but definitely not God; they reduce Jesus to a good man or a mere prophet. Most of us realize that false religions teach such diabolical ungodliness, but even some mainline churches today no longer believe in the inerrancy of the Word of God or in the Jesus of the

Bible. They take the parts of the Bible that they like and dismiss other parts with which they disagree.

I recently read a story about a person who left a mainline denominational church when she was a young child because the church was pro-life. This individual is pro-choice. But my question is: How did she know that she was pro-choice at age six; who told her that she was pro-choice? Adults who are pro-choice certainly don't know the Jesus of the Bible. They have a Jesus whom they have created in their own image, and they believe a gospel they themselves have authored.

In spite of many people and churches rejecting Jesus and the Word of God, Jesus is still God who came in the flesh to redeem mankind, and the Word of God is still valid today. Every word in the Scriptures is God-breathed whether people believe the Word of God or not, and unmistakably, Jesus is God. Although at least one false religion indicates that Jesus never claimed to be God, it's clear that Jesus stated His divine nature numerous times. This made the religious leaders of His time very angry and is one reason they wanted to kill Him. They wouldn't accept Jesus as God, which is one of the reasons that the religious and political leaders eventually crucified Him. The religious crowd knew Jesus claimed to be God, but they wouldn't accept His divinity.

Many priests and religious folks in the first century looked for Jesus and the fulfillment of Old Testament prophecy, but most of them didn't recognize Him when He finally appeared on earth. Most of them either didn't recognize Him or were too ungodly to accept Him as the Messiah. A lot of people are still like that today; they simply either don't recognize Jesus or won't accept Him. He doesn't meet their preconceived notion of who Jesus should be, nor do they approve of who Jesus really is. Most people want to live their lives unhindered by Jesus Christ. Jesus must conform to their likes and dislikes, or He isn't welcome in their lives.

Most people are too arrogant to accept Jesus on His terms, so many either claim He isn't God or just ignore Him altogether. Multiple Scriptures absolutely confirm the identity of Jesus—Jesus Christ is God. Colossians 1:15–16 states: "He is the image of the invisible God, the firstborn over all creation. For by Him all things were created that are in heaven and that are on earth." Various Scriptures beginning in Genesis and continuing through the last book of the Bible show Jesus as the Creator.

Genesis 1:1 says: "In the beginning God created the heavens and the earth." John 1:3 tells us that all things were made by Him (referring to Jesus). Question: If the Bible tells us that God created all things and at the same time tells us that Jesus created all things, then who is Jesus? The answer can only be that Jesus is God!

First Timothy 3:16 states: "And without controversy great is the mystery of godliness: God was manifested in the flesh, justified in the Spirit, seen by angels, preached among the Gentiles, believed on in the world, received up in glory." This Scripture clearly is referring to Jesus. So this is yet another Scripture declaring that Jesus is almighty God!

Some individuals argue that Jesus admitted that He wasn't God in a conversation with the rich young ruler identified in the gospels of Matthew, Mark, and Luke. Nothing could be further from the truth. That was not what Jesus was saying at all! Jesus wanted the rich young ruler to acknowledge Him as God, and to accept the gift of salvation.

The young ruler was careful to keep all of the religious laws, but he didn't recognize Jesus as the Messiah. He addressed Jesus as "Good Teacher." Jesus asked him why he had called Him good, since nobody is good except God. Jesus was challenging the rich young ruler to acknowledge Him as God, but the young man failed to recognize Jesus for who He was. If the ruler had exclaimed, "Jesus, I called You good because You are God," Jesus would have said, "You are right, well said, now come and follow Me and be My disciple." If the young man had acknowledged Jesus for who He really was, then Jesus would not have admonished him to sell what he owned and give it to the poor in order to be perfect (see Matthew 19:21).

Further proof that Jesus is God is recorded in the story located in Mark 2:5–7. In this particular story, Jesus spoke to a paralytic man telling him that his sins were forgiven, thus revealing that He had power to forgive people's sins. Some of the unbelieving scribes thought Jesus was blaspheming, because they knew that **only** God has the ability to forgive sins.

The book of Hebrews, written specifically to the Jewish people, has a number of verses reflecting that Jesus is God. In Hebrews 1:8, the Father says to Jesus: "Your throne, O God, is forever and ever; a scepter of righteousness is the scepter of Your kingdom." In Hebrews 1:10, God continues to address Jesus: "You, LORD, in the beginning laid the foundation of the earth, and the heavens are the work of Your hands."

Again, if the Scriptures say God created the heavens and the earth, and if the Father says that Jesus created them—then who is Jesus? God the Father says Jesus is God. The Scriptures say that Jesus is God. The apostles of Jesus said that Jesus is God, and Jesus Himself claimed to be God. So, one can only come to one logical and spiritual conclusion concerning Jesus—and that is that Jesus is God.

By the way, the Holy Spirit also is God. There is only one God—God the Father, God the Son, and God the Holy Spirit. This is a difficult concept for many human beings to fully understand. It sort of helps to look at the personalities of a person; the same person can be a son, a father, and a husband, but he is still only one person, not multiple persons. Also, individuals are body, soul, and spirit. These, of course, are poor examples, but it's the best I can do.

Again, it's difficult for most people to grasp the concept of one God in three persons. Many false religions deny that Jesus is God, and many of them also deny that the Holy Spirit is God.

30

PROGRESSIVE CHRISTIANITY?

EVERYTHING ABOUT PROGRESSIVE CHRISTIANITY IS FALSE doctrine—ABSOLUTELY EVERYTHING. There is not a single ounce of truth in progressive thinking and teaching, and there is no such thing as Christianity that is progressive.

The terms *progressive* and *Christian* are misnomers. There is radically progressive thinking, but the individuals promoting this worldview aren't Christians. They are under the sway of the devil and are motivated by the evil one to deny the Jesus of the Bible and inerrancy of God's Word. Progressive Christianity has divorced itself from the authority of the Scriptures in order to embrace the radical ideology of the culture.

Anyone believing in progressive theology is badly deceived and is under a curse. We are alerted over and over again in the

Scriptures not to allow ourselves to be deceived. Colossians 2:8 warns: "See to it that no one takes you captive through philosophy and empty deception, according to the tradition of men, according to the elementary principles of the world, rather than according to Christ" (NASB).

First John 5:19 states: "We know that we are of God, and the whole world lies under the sway of the wicked one." This Scripture states that all Christians belong to God, but sinners are under the influence of the devil.

Paul warns in the book of Galatians that anyone teaching another gospel other than that contained in the Scriptures is accursed. Galatians 1:8 says: "But even if we, or an angel from heaven, preach any other gospel to you than what we have preached to you, let him be accursed." We are warned by the apostle Paul about the spiritual condition of people and churches in the last days. First Timothy 4:1 states: "Now the Spirit expressly says that in latter times some will depart from the faith, giving heed to deceiving spirits and doctrines of demons."

Progressive Christianity teaches doctrines of demons, including universalism and hyper social justice. The social justice portion of progressive Christianity has made inroads into some *so-called* Christian churches today. People must not be deceived by false doctrine and false teachers. People need to reject this kind of diabolical teaching, because souls of individuals depend upon rejecting false theology. Also, people need to avoid liberal churches that ordain ungodly ministers, cause racial division, promote abortion, teach a perverted version of inclusion, or preach anything that grossly violates clear teachings of Scripture.

31

DAYS OF NOAH OR A HUGE SPIRITUAL AWAKENING?

MOST CHRISTIANS AGREE WE'RE LIVING IN THE *VERY LAST* OF the last days. There is a lot of debate, however, as to what will be taking place on the earth immediately prior to either the rapture of the Christian church or the Second Advent of Jesus Christ. Some theologians believe that the darkness now enveloping the whole world will dissipate, people will repent of their wicked ways, and there will be a great spiritual revival that will usher in the rapture of the Church. Other theologians believe the world will grow darker and darker, and the entire earth will be overwhelmed with such evil that we will be living in days like those experienced by Noah and his family just prior to the flood that was sent by God to destroy mankind and cleanse the earth of unrighteousness.

Individuals believing in a great spiritual awakening base their theology on Scriptures indicating that God will pour out His Spirit on all people. For instance, the Lord indicates in Isaiah 44:3 that He will pour out His Spirit upon the descendants of Israel. In Zechariah 12:10, the Lord promises to pour out the Spirit of grace upon the descendants of King David. Then again in Joel 2:28, the Lord uses the prophet Joel to proclaim to the kingdom of Judah that He will pour out His Spirit on all flesh. All three of these proclamations from the Lord are addressed to the Jewish people, to occur at some future date.

Jesus told His disciples in Luke 24:49 to wait in Jerusalem until He sent the promise of His Father, and they would be endued with power from on high. The promise of the Father was that He would pour out His Spirit upon all believers, both Jews and Gentiles. This didn't mean that every person on earth would be filled with the Holy Spirit, but only believers would be filled with the Spirit of God.

In Acts 1:4–7, Jesus again promises His disciples that they will receive power when the Holy Spirit has come upon them. The disciples assembled together in Jerusalem on the Day of Pentecost, and indeed they were all filled with the Holy Spirit (Acts 2:1–4). The apostle Peter later proclaimed in Acts 2:16 that this was what previously had been spoken by the prophet Joel. Joel 2:28 states: "And it shall come to pass afterward that I will pour out My Spirit on all flesh; Your sons and your daughters shall prophesy, your old men shall dream dreams, your young men shall see visions." Clearly, Peter believed that Joel 2:28 was being fulfilled when the Holy Spirit was poured out upon the believers gathered in Jerusalem to wait for the promise.

What do the words mean: "It shall come to pass afterward"? I believe the words mean that *after* Jesus is crucified, resurrected, and goes back to heaven that the Holy Spirit will be poured out upon people. This is exactly what took place in the book of Acts, and Peter indicated that what previously had been promised by God happened just as He had promised. Then to ensure that no one could misinterpret what the apostle Peter meant, he restated the prophecy of Joel 2:28 in Acts 2:17.

Many theologians believe this outpouring on the Day of Pentecost in Jerusalem was only a partial fulfillment of Joel's prophecy. They teach that there will be a greater outpouring of the Holy Spirit as we get closer to the return of Christ. Some ministers also teach that the Lord has saved the ***best*** wine for last based on the miracle performed by Jesus at the wedding of Cana (John 2:1–10). It's possible, however, that the greatest outpouring of God's Spirit has already occurred, and that the best wine has already been provided.

Jesus told His disciples that it was better for Him to go away and for Him to send the Holy Spirit in His place. To me, the Holy Spirit signifies the best wine that has been poured out upon believers for the past two thousand years.

The Scriptures seem to indicate that the world will grow darker, and that people will grow more corrupt as time advances toward the return of Christ (see Isaiah 60:2 and Matthew 24:3–39). We are told that perilous times will exist and that deception will be rampant in the last days. The Bible also warns about people calling evil good and good evil (Isaiah 5:20). That is certainly happening today!

When the disciples asked Christ what would be the sign of His coming and the end of the age, Jesus painted a very bleak picture about what would be occurring upon the earth just prior to His return. In fact, Jesus told His disciples that things would be so dire that, if possible, even the elect would be deceived. Jesus described a lot of calamity taking place upon the earth, but He never mentioned a huge spiritual revival. In fact, Jesus indicated that the spiritual condition of people will be like that of those living in the days of Noah. That's not a very lovely picture!

The Scriptures seem to reflect individuals becoming more corrupt, not experiencing a spiritual awakening. I don't see in the Word of God where spiritual darkness and revival occur simultaneously just prior to the return of Jesus. I know this could happen, and I'm aware that many modern prophets have prophesied that a huge spiritual awakening will sweep across the entire world soon. I may be a bit cynical, but most of the prophecies of modern-day prophets never come to pass. So, I'm not holding my breath for these prophecies to manifest. I choose to search the Scriptures in order to determine future events.

Again, the Scriptures seem to indicate that morality will continue to grow worse—resembling that in the days of Noah. In those days, things got so bad that God decided to destroy mankind with a flood, sparing only Noah and his family. The Lord gave Noah 120 years to build an ark for safety. This also allowed time for people to repent. Noah preached for 120 years to the people residing on the earth in those days, but Noah didn't get a single convert. Instead, he was mocked and belittled by those whom he tried to convert. If Noah preached to the politicians in our nation's capital today, I would be surprised if he had any converts.

Rather than debate whether we'll be living in a time like the days of Noah or during a spiritual revival at the end of the age, let us consider our own spiritual condition to ensure we are ready for the return of Christ. I encourage people to follow the advice found in 2 Corinthians 13:5, which states: "Examine yourselves to see whether you are in the faith; test yourselves. Do you not realize that Christ Jesus is in you—unless, of course, you fail the test?" (NIV).

In an age of much deception, individuals need to definitively determine that they genuinely know the Lord Jesus Christ. I sincerely hope that there will be a great spiritual awakening in our country and around the world. But I must confess that I'm not sure that will happen. I'm unsure if modern prophets and evangelists have heard from the Lord about revival or if they are just subjects of wishful thinking. One thing we can know for sure: If there's a major spiritual awakening soon, then that means that the Second Advent of Christ most likely won't happen in our lifetime. The Scriptures are clear that Jesus Christ will return in an era not unlike that in the days of Noah.

NOTE: Lest anyone accuse God of wrongdoing by sending the flood, let me explain His purpose. People were so corrupt in those days that only eight people were saved (Noah, his wife, his three sons, and Noah's three daughters-in-law). Had God not chosen to destroy virtually all people and start over with the human race being repopulated by Noah's family, then no one could have been saved. Mankind was so corrupted that it would have been impossible for Jesus to have been born of a virgin centuries later. Without Jesus, no one would have been saved. The Lord God always knows what He is doing. He can foresee the future that we cannot see. Blessed be the name of the Lord.

CONCLUSION

SOME OF THE FALSE DOCTRINE I HAVE OUTLINED IN THIS BOOK is dangerous, while other false teachings simply are questionable or a bit silly. My intent in exposing these theological concepts isn't to cause division or turn anyone off to the Gospel. While we would be wise to avoid false doctrine, apostate churches, and flawed prophets, it wouldn't be wise to distrust Jesus or discount true Christian churches. The Lord is not responsible for the ungodly behavior or sometimes nonsensical beliefs of some Christians. The Scriptures, when interpreted correctly, can be trusted to provide truth, and the Lord Jesus Christ can be trusted to provide eternal life.

I know in the past that several individuals supposedly have lost their faith, because they put too much confidence in a particular minister or prophet. This in itself is a false doctrine. We are never to trust wholly in mankind, but we're to place our complete faith and trust in our Lord Jesus Christ. Jesus has promised to never leave us or forsake us, and Jesus can be trusted with our future and with telling us the complete, uncompromised truth.

People, no matter how godly, will sometimes fail or disappoint us. We aren't to put our faith in flawed men or women. Many *so-called* prophets predicted that President Trump would win reelection in

2020 by a landslide and that the evil people opposing him would be exposed and brought to justice. Other prophets claimed that the election results would go to the Supreme Court and that the justices would rule in Trump's favor. As we all know, this didn't happen! Either these prophets proclaimed themselves to be prophets, or they expressed wishful thinking—or they simply prophesied lies in order to attain invitations on Christian television shows.

I heard some confused folks say that these prophets had made them totally distrust Christianity and caused them to completely lose their faith in Christ. This is extremely sad and unfortunate, and it should be a warning to individuals not to trust too heavily in unproven people. I have felt let down and very disappointed at times by some of the ministries that I have supported financially for many years, but I won't allow them to interfere with my faith in Christ. Christians often let us down. Only **Jesus** can be trusted to **never disappoint** us. Jesus can be trusted to be a Friend who never disappoints—plus faith in Him guarantees eternal life.

If you have already accepted Jesus as your Savior, then I encourage you to become a student of the Word and make disciples of other individuals. If your faith has been put on hold or diminished by imperfect people, choose to forgive them and retrieve your faith. But if you don't know Jesus, now would be a good time to repent and ask Jesus to save you. Also, ask the Holy Spirit to illuminate the Scriptures to you as you read the Bible. I recommend reading the New King James Version. I also advise you to ask the Holy Spirit to help you find a good church where the *true* Gospel is being preached. Knowing Jesus as your Savior is the most important decision you will ever make in your life. May the Lord richly bless you, give you His peace, and prepare you for His Kingdom that is to come.